# THE FAMILY
# Easter Book

### Alan MacDonald

A LION BOOK
Oxford · Batavia · Sydney

Published by
**Lion Publishing**
1705 Hubbard Avenue, Batavia, IL 60510 USA
ISBN 0 7459 2349 6

First edition 1993

**Acknowledgments**
Cassell plc, 'Hurray for Jesus', page 50, from *Someone's Singing,
Lord* by Sister Oswin
Carol Watson, 'A Prayer for Lent', page 60, from *365 Children's
Prayers*, Lion Publishing
Iona Miller, 'Dear Lord, thank you', page 61, from *365 Children's
Prayers*, Lion Publishing
Cowley Publications, 'Christ, we thank you', page 61, from *Plain
Prayers for a Complicated World*
Rachel Hartley, 'E is for Easter', and Elaine Round, 'Dear God,
Thank you', page 62, from *The Lion Book of Family Prayers*, Lion
Publishing
Macmillan Publishers Ltd, 'The Ballad of the Bread Man', page 81,
from *Collected Poems* by Charles Causley

**Picture acknowledgments**
Andes Press Agency/Carlos Reyes: 75, 85; Neil Beer: 90/91; Lion
Publishing: 8, 9, 10/11, 19, 67; Lion Publishing/David Townsend:
68; Mansell Collection: 59; National Film Archive: 46; National
Portrait Gallery, London: 57; Press Association/Topham: 34; Willi
Rauch: 86; Rex Features: 58; Topham: 12; John Williams: 32, 37, 38,
39, 40; World Pictures: 45; ZEFA: 23, 27, 31, 77, 78.

Library of Congress CIP data applied for

Printed and bound in Malaysia

# Contents

# *What Does Easter Mean Today?*

Ring out the bells—Easter is here! It's a time for holidays, games and festivals; a time for giving Easter eggs, hard-boiled, chocolate or beautifully hand-painted. But Easter is much more. It is the oldest and most important Christian festival, the celebration of the death and coming to life again of Jesus Christ. Easter is the astonishing end to the story that begins with Christmas.

At the heart of the December festival is Jesus the babe in a manger; at the heart of Easter is Jesus the man, his death on the cross and triumph over the grave. Without Easter it's doubtful that we would still celebrate Christmas at all. Christ's birth would not be much remembered if his life had ended on Good Friday in the grave. For Christians therefore, the dawn of Easter Sunday with its message of new life is the high point of the year.

## ORIGINS

How did it start? Like most festivals, Easter has its origins in pre-Christian times. Our ancestors believed that the sun died in winter and was born anew in spring. Winter was a time of hardship and hunger, when trees and fields were bare and animals were hibernating. When the days started to lengthen and the sun regained its warmth and power, the spring festival was a cause for great celebration.

Different gods—the Roman Attis and the Eastern Adonis—were thanked for bringing the earth back to life. In Europe the goddess Eostre was credited with the arrival of spring and many believe it was she who lent

# EASTER DATES AND THEIR MEANINGS

Unlike Christmas, which is celebrated by the Western churches on December 25 every year, the date of Easter varies. Easter Day is always a Sunday, and since the fourth century Western churches have celebrated Easter on the Sunday following the first full moon after the Spring equinox. This rather odd method of calculation resulted from hot disputes among different branches of the church more than 1600 years ago!

In practice, this means that Easter can fall as early as March 22 or as late as April 25.

There are many special days during both the Easter festival and the forty day period of preparation for Easter known as Lent. The last week in Lent, beginning on Palm Sunday, is called Holy Week.

### Shrove Tuesday
The last day before Lent begins. In the Middle Ages people were called to church to be 'shriven' (have their sins forgiven) as a preparation for Lent.

### Ash Wednesday
The first day of Lent. Ash from the burning of last year's palm crosses from Palm Sunday is used to mark people's foreheads with a cross in some churches.

### Mothering Sunday (Mother's Day)
In Britain and in many other European countries, this day comes in mid-Lent. A special day for mothers or for the 'mother' church that people attend.

### Palm Sunday
When Jesus rode into Jerusalem and the people spread palm leaves in his path to welcome him.

### Maundy Thursday
From the Latin *maundatum* meaning command. The Last Supper is remembered when Jesus washed his disciples' feet and gave a new commandment to love one another as he had loved them.

### Good Friday
When Jesus was crucified. The name may be derived from 'God's Friday'.

### Easter Sunday
The day Christians celebrate Jesus rising from the dead.

her name to our festival of Easter.

The word for Easter in most European countries comes from the Greek *Pasch*, which means Passover. The Passover is the feast when the Jews remember their flight from captivity in Egypt. It is also the time when Christ was crucified.

Easter and spring don't always go together. In countries of the southern hemisphere, Easter falls near the end of autumn. But the world over, Easter is felt to be a time of new life and new beginnings because of Jesus' rebirth.

It isn't hard to see why the early Christians felt the spring festival was especially fitting to celebrate Easter. Jesus himself pointed to the lesson of nature that all things must die in order to be reborn to new life:

*Unless an ear of wheat falls into the ground and dies, it remains only a single seed. But if it dies it produces many seeds.*
**The Gospel of John**

Many of our Easter traditions still echo this truth. The sun rising on Easter morning, the newborn chick breaking from its shell, the light of a candle banishing the darkness around, all point to the joyful news of Jesus' resurrection.

## ENTER THE KING

During Easter we look back on the events known as Holy Week when Jesus entered into the great city of Jerusalem and was arrested and put to death. Almost everyone knows that Jesus was born in a manger in Bethlehem and died on a cross, but why are people still remembering this 2000 years later?

Our records of Jesus' life are based mainly on the four Gospels, eyewitness accounts set down by those who knew Jesus or his disciples so that no one should be in any doubt about the facts. None of the Gospel writers spends much time on Jesus' early life. It's as if they are eager to hurry on

# WHO WAS JESUS?

People of all races and creeds have been fascinated by the character of Jesus for centuries. Today, more than one third of the world's population claim to be his followers. But whom are they following?

Jesus left his followers in little doubt about his identity.

### Who Jesus said he was

◇ Jesus claimed to be the Son of God—not just one of God's children but his only son.

◇ Jesus claimed to be the Messiah—the one the Jewish people hoped would come to save Israel.

◇ Jesus allowed his followers to call him Lord—this put him on a par with God.

◇ Jesus said he could forgive the wrong things that people had done—according to Jewish teaching, only God could do that.

after the story of the birth to the dramatic last three years of Jesus' life, and in particular, the last few days.

## The story so far

Luke sets the opening scene of these last three years in a parched and barren desert—the wilderness. Jesus chooses this desolate place to prepare himself for his mission to the people of Israel by rejecting temptations to go about it the wrong way. Soon he has gathered a group of twelve followers—including fishermen, tax collectors and political activists—and begins to tour the villages around Galilee.

Jesus is like no teacher there has been before. He mixes with beggars, prostitutes and the detested tax collectors. He treats women as equals and talks about God as his own father. Then there are his astonishing miracles: a blind man sees, a lame man walks, and on one startling occasion a funeral is interrupted when Jesus commands the dead man to get up from his grave.

Not surprisingly, people start to flock to

Jesus in every village—some to see miracles, others to hear him speak. Jesus teaches them in stories—about a father who welcomes home a runaway, a shepherd who searches for a lost sheep, and a king who throws a great party for the poor and disabled. These are pictures of God, he says, who is only waiting for our move in order to forgive and receive us. .

But not everyone is pleased. Some of the Jewish church leaders are jealous of Jesus' popularity and fear his influence with the people. It is whispered that if he dares to set foot in Jerusalem, they will have him arrested and executed.

Against this background the Jewish Passover arrives, and Jesus announces his intention to celebrate the feast in Jerusalem. His followers' protests are brushed aside and they begin the long walk to the great city with fear in their hearts . . .

# LENT—A TIME TO TAKE STOCK

'What are you giving up for Lent?' Not so many years ago this was the question adults and children asked each other on Ash Wednesday, the first day of Lent. Nowadays not many people in the West make Lent a special time for self-denial. But where did the idea come from in the first place?

No one is sure where the word Lent comes from. It could be from the Anglo Saxon *lencten*, meaning spring, or the German word *lenz*, which conveys the time of year when the days lengthen. Traditionally, Lent looks back to the time when Jesus spent forty days in the wilderness without food, so it lasts for forty days from Ash Wednesday to Easter Eve. This is actually forty-six days, but the six Sundays are not counted, because Sunday is the day when Jesus rose from the dead, and hence a day to celebrate, even in Lent.

## The beginnings of Lent

In the early years of the church, a period of fasting—going without food—was originally kept from Easter Eve to 3 am on Easter morning, since it was thought that Christ rose from the dead at that time of day. Later the fast was extended to include the forty days of Lent. For the early Christians, Easter was the time when new believers were baptized into membership of the church. Lent was used as a time of preparation. New Christians learned the essentials of the Christian faith and examined their lives in the light of Jesus' teaching. Committed Christians also took Lent seriously, spending time in prayer and meditation.

These days, ideas about Lent have become rather confused. It is sometimes thought of as a time for sacrifice and general mournfulness. Giving up chocolate or coffee for forty days may be good for the body, but it is only a pale shadow of what Lent is really about.

It is more accurate to think of Lent as a time for taking stock, a spiritual spring cleaning to prepare for the joy of Easter. A traditional English song, *White Lent*, makes the point:

*To bow the head*
*In sackcloth and in ashes*
*Or to afflict the soul,*
*Such grief is not Lent's goal*
*But to be led*
*To where God's glory flashes.*

## Lenten customs

In the Orthodox church, Lent is still kept more strictly. In countries such as Poland and the Ukraine, only certain foods are eaten. A Lenten meal in the Ukraine might include vegetables, fruit, honey and a special bread; meat and dairy products are forbidden. The fourth Wednesday in Lent is Middle Cross Day, celebrated by eating cakes baked in the shape of a cross. In Greece the first day of Lent is a holiday known as Clean Monday. In all the villages and towns it is the signal for an outing to the countryside. Families set out for the fields and woods carrying large hampers of food and bottles of wine. The children hold bright kites which they fly as an essential part of the Clean Monday celebrations.

## Shrove Tuesday

Shrove Tuesday, now frequently referred to as Pancake Day, is the day before Ash Wednesday. In the days when Lent was strictly observed as a time of fasting, Shrove Tuesday was the day when feasting and merry-making was the rule.

On that day, people were called to church to confess their sins and be 'shriven'

(forgiven) before Lent began. Eggs were among the forbidden foods of the Lenten season, so one way to use them up was to cook pancakes.

In Britain, Shrove Tuesday was sometimes called 'goodies day' and the bell that called the faithful to church was known as the pancake bell. But it was not only pancakes that were on offer, as a traditional verse of 1684 hints:

> *But hark I hear the pancake bell*
> *And fritters make a gallant smell;*
> *The cooks are baking, frying, boyling,*
> *Stewing, mincing, cutting, broyling,*
> *Carving, gormandising, roasting,*
> *Carbonading, cracking, slashing,*
>     *toasting.*
> **From** *Poor Robin's Alamanack*

All kinds of strange customs are associated with Shrove Tuesday. One is the annual pancake race held in the town of Olney in England. The story goes that it started in 1445 when a housewife who was late cooking her pancakes heard the church bell and ran to church taking her griddle and batter along with her.

Ever since, the Olney pancake race has been held, involving women who must run from the town square to the church, tossing a pancake in their pan at least three times along the route. In 1950 the race gained an international dimension when housewives in Liberal, Kansas, challenged their Olney counterparts. The winners' times were compared by transatlantic telephone.

In Sweden the day is known as Fat Tuesday. The dish of the day is the Fat Tuesday bun which is filled with almond paste and whipped cream and served floating in a bowl of hot milk.

In Belgium, children enjoy an Easter version of carol singing. They are rewarded with nuts, apples and strips of bacon which should traditionally be cooked outdoors on long willow sticks.

Perhaps the strangest custom of all originated with the Dutch farmers of

Zeeland. It involved taking their horses, splendidly groomed and bedecked with paper roses, down to the beach to wet their hooves in the sea. This symbol of cleansing was followed by a feast back at the village.

## PERFECT PANCAKES (MAKES 12)

### You need:

◇ ²/₃ cup plain flour  ◇ A pinch of salt
◇ 2 eggs  ◇ 1 tbsp oil
◇ 1¼ cups milk  ◇ Cooking fat

### To make:

1 Sieve the flour and salt into a bowl.

2 Make a well in the middle and pour in the eggs. Add half the milk gradually and beat well to give a sticky consistency. Mix in the remaining milk. Stir in the oil just before cooking.

3 Melt a little fat in the pan, just enough to cover the base. Let the fat get very hot and nearly smoking. Use about two spoonsful of batter for each pancake, tipping pan to spread it thinly.

4 Cook at medium heat for about two minutes until light brown underneath. Turn with a spatula, or toss (see above) to cook other side.

5 Keep cooked pancakes on a hot covered dish.

# MAKING ROOM FOR EASTER

The early Christians who set aside the weeks leading up to Easter for prayer and reflection had good reasons. They knew that life is busy and the days speed past, running into years before you know it. Time to take stock, to reassess the balance of your life and your priorities, is hard to find.

Whether or not we share the same motivation as the early Christians, we can all benefit from a time to take stock. Easter is a time to clear away the old and make room for the new. There may be things we would like to change or we may just want to 'count our blessings'. Once we stop to look around us there is still plenty in the world to be thankful for, despite all that is evil and unjust.

*I will thank him for the pleasures*
*given me through my senses,*
*For the glory of the thunder,*
*For the mystery of music,*
*The singing of the birds*
*And the laughter of children.*
*I will thank him for the pleasures of*
*seeing,*

*For the delights through colour,*
*The awe of the sunset,*
*The beauty of flowers,*
*The smile of friendship*
*And the look of love;*
*For the changing beauty of the*
*clouds,*
*For the wild roses in the hedges,*
*For the form and the beauty of the*
*birds,*
*For the leaves on the trees in spring*
*and autumn,*
*For the witness of the trees through*
*the winter*
*Teaching us that death is sleep and*
*not destruction . . .*
*Truly O Lord, the earth is full of thy*
*riches.*

**Edward King, Bishop of Lincoln**
**(1829–1910)**

Serve with lemon and sugar, honey or maple syrup, or roll and add delicious fruit fillings.

### To toss a pancake:

6  Shake the pan before attempting to toss. The pancake should move freely if it is cooked.

7  Hold the pan loosely with your wrist relaxed and facing downwards. Give the pan a sharp flick upwards and be ready to catch your pancake as it flips over and lands!

# M O T H E R I N G
# S U N D A Y

In many European countries the fourth Sunday in Lent is set aside as a special day to honor mothers.

In England, Mothering Sunday originally had a different meaning. It was the day when church-goers in outlying villages and hamlets would make the journey to the mother church of the parish, taking their offerings.

## Simnel cakes and sweethearts

By the sixteenth century, when many young girls worked as servants in the homes of the rich, Mothering Sunday had become a holiday when they were allowed home to visit their families.

To prove their newly-acquired skills in the kitchen, they would bake a cake to present proudly to their mothers. It was called a simnel cake, probably from the Latin word *simila*, a fine wheat flour. The cake was usually made with a rich mixture filled with plums, lemon peel and other tasty ingredients. It had to last until Easter, as it couldn't be eaten until after Lent had passed.

If a girl had a sweetheart, Mothering Sunday was the day to bring him home for mother's approval. In this case it was the man's responsibility to provide the mothering cake.

In more modern times, Mother's Day was introduced and is still kept in America and Australia on the second Sunday in May. The idea is attributed to Anna Jarvis of Philadelphia who, in 1907, suggested an annual day for mothers should be kept. At a church service people were asked to wear a white carnation as a tribute to their mother. The custom soon became known and spread to other places.

# MAKE MOTHER'S DAY!

**Mother's Day today is still a time when children can show their mother that they appreciate all that she does for them. Flowers are one popular gift to give with a card. With a little help, you can give both by making a beautiful paper flower card.**

## FLOWERING CARD

### You need:

◇ Colored card 8 x 14in., folded in half
◇ Two sheets of different colored tissue paper (for example two shades of pink) 6 x 18in.
◇ Small scissors
◇ Glue
◇ Paper fastener

### To make:

1  First fold each sheet of tissue into three equal squares. Cut out until you have six squares 6 x 6in.

The three darker shade squares are for the outer petals, the lighter shade will make the inner petals.

2  Take a tissue square, fold it in half diagonally, in half again and in half a third time until you have a small triangle.

3  Then work the triangle into a cone shape.

4  Repeat with each of the other tissue squares.

5  Next cut out the shape of the petals. For the outside petals cut a single rounded edge. For the inside petals cut a double edge.

6  Now you can open out your petals. Stick the three outside petals down on the front of your card with a small dab of glue in the center of each. Then stick the three inside petals on top in the same way.

7  Secure carefully with a paper fastener through the middle of the flower. Push it through the card and fasten at the back.

8  Gently shape the flower by separating the petals and curling the inside petals upwards. Write your message to Mother inside the card.

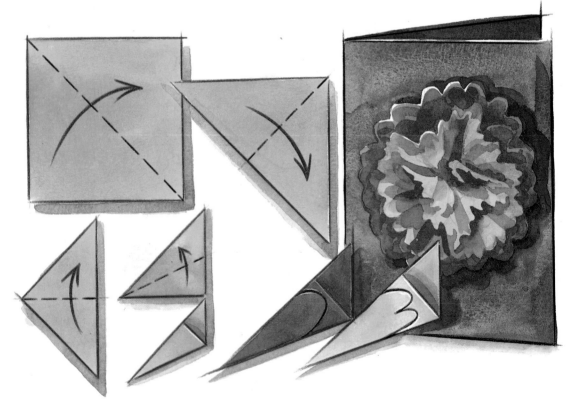

# Welcome the Festival

*When Jesus entered Jerusalem, the whole city was thrown into an uproar. 'Who is he?' the people asked.*

**The Gospel of Matthew**

**The Sunday before Easter is known as Palm Sunday. This celebrates the momentous occasion when Jesus entered Jerusalem. Great crowds of people thronged the streets waving palm branches to welcome him. Imagine being in Jerusalem on that day, like the small boy who tells this story . . .**

## The king who rode a donkey

When we reached the city walls there were crowds already there. I knew lots of visitors were in Jerusalem for the Passover but I'd never seen so many people before. Everyone was talking and craning their necks to see along the road that runs past the Mount of Olives.

'They're coming!' somebody shouted, 'I can see them!'

People started to push forward excitedly. My Uncle Silas hoisted me up onto his shoulders so that I didn't get knocked over.

'What can you see?' he asked.

There was a crowd entering the city gate. Many were holding palm leaves and waving them in the air like banners. Other people had taken off their cloaks and were spreading them down on the road as the procession reached them. The noise of shouting and cheering was almost deafening. In the middle of the procession was a small grey donkey. A man sat on his back smiling at the children who ran along-side him as they patted the donkey and laughed.

'Praise God!' shouted a woman next to me. 'Blessed is he who comes in the name of the Lord!'

Soon everyone was shouting and cheering. A man climbed into a tree and threw down palm branches; I caught one and waved it till my arm ached. Uncle Silas was hopping from foot to foot trying to get a better view and making it difficult for me to stay on his shoulders. The man on the donkey kept on smiling and watching everyone as he went past. Soon the procession had gone, heading towards the middle of Jerusalem.

'The time is upon us, Simeon,' said Uncle Silas on our way home. 'This Jesus will be the one to save us, you'll see.'

# THE HUMBLE DONKEY

Donkeys are usually thought of as slow, stubborn, beasts of burden which lack the grace or intelligence of horses. So why should Jesus deliberately have chosen a donkey to ride into Jerusalem?

The answer is probably connected with people's expectations of the coming Messiah. For a long time the Jews had been living in hope of the Messiah coming, a king descended from David who would deliver them and usher in a new era for Israel.

In the Old Testament the coming of the future king is predicted in these words:

> *He comes triumphant and victorious, but humble and riding on a donkey—*
> *on a colt, the foal of a donkey.*

So Jesus was fulfilling the role of Messiah by riding into Jersualem on a colt. But he was also upsetting the expectations of many Jews. They saw the Messiah as a political figure, a nationalist leader who would overthrow the Romans and restore Israel to the Jews. By making his entry on a donkey, Jesus demonstrated that he was a king bringing a message of peace— not a rebel commander riding his horse into battle.

# CARDS FOR EASTER

In many countries people send cards to wish each other a happy Easter. This year, why not surprise friends or family by making your own Easter cards? Here are three simple-to-make designs.

## FUNNY BUNNIES

### You need:

◇ Colored card 16 x 4¼ in.
◇ Cotton balls
◇ Scissors
◇ Felt pen

### To make:

1  Accordion-fold the card three times.

2  Draw round the bunny template with the nose and tail touching the folded edges of the card. Cut out the shape taking care to leave the folded edges intact.

3  Pull out the garland of bunnies. Add a finishing touch by sticking on cotton tails and drawing an eye on each bunny.

## EGGSHELL MOSAIC

**Painted eggshell can be used to make a mosaic in any simple design. Try making an Easter cross or a rising sun as a reminder of Jesus rising to life on Easter Sunday.**

### You need:

◇ 6 eggshells broken into large pieces
◇ A piece of stiff card
◇ Wallpaper paste and gluebrush
◇ Poster paints and brush

### To make:

1 Cut the card to the size you want and fold in half.

2 Draw your design first onto paper for practice. Then copy it onto the front of the card using bold lines.

3 Wash and dry the eggshells and break into large pieces. Arrange them on your design so that you can see how many pieces are needed in each color. Remove them and paint with bright poster paints. Leave to dry.

4 Make up a thick wallpaper paste and brush it carefully all over the design.

5 Gently place the eggshells onto the pasted surface in your design. Leave to dry.

## EGGCITING EASTER

**A bright Easter egg card can be made with wrapping paper.**

### You need:

◇ A sheet of bright wrapping paper (for example spots or flowers)
◇ Colored card
◇ Colored ribbon
◇ Scissors

### To make:

1 Fold the colored card in two.

2 Draw an egg shape on the wrapping paper. Cut it out and stick it down on the front of your card.

3 To add the ribbon, make two slits either side of the egg and pass a piece of ribbon through. Tie in a bow at the front.

4 Write your own greeting, such as 'Have an Eggciting Easter!'

# EASTER ON PARADE

When Jesus entered into Jerusalem on the first Palm Sunday, crowds cheered and waved palm branches. It really was the first Easter procession. Nowadays the Easter season is a time for carnivals and processions all over the world.

## Mardi Gras

The word carnival actually means 'farewell to the flesh' which is why many carnivals take place just before the beginning of Lent. Since overeating, singing and dancing used to be forbidden during the Lent season, people wanted to have one last big feast before it began! Perhaps the best known carnival is Mardi Gras, (literally 'Fat Tuesday'), which often takes place on Shrove Tuesday. In New Orleans in the United States of America it is such a big event that it lasts for six days. No one knows precisely how Mardi Gras started, but the first revellers were said to be students returning to New Orleans from Paris who danced through the French quarter wearing weird masks and costumes. According to one observer; 'He who tastes of Mardi Gras will also return. It's the maddest, fastest, giddiest, most absurd, most magnificent thing in New Orleans.'

## Caribbean carnival

Mardi Gras is also celebrated in the Caribbean islands of Trinidad and Tobago. The beginning of Carnival is announced with a rocket on the Sunday morning before Lent, known as *Dimanche Gras*, when the king and queen of Carnival are crowned. The following day is *Jouvray*, a day and night of dancing.

On Mardi Gras itself the calypso singers and musicans take over the streets with costume bands that can involve as many as 2000 people! Several traditional characters always appear in the carnival: Moco Jumbie walking on tall stilts, Jab Molassi who threatens to smear the crowd with the sticky

molasses covering him from head to foot, and Burroquite who wears a donkey costume.

## Brazil

South America also boasts claimants to the title of the greatest carnival on earth. In Brazil the four days before Lent are a time of almost continuous parades, balls and revels. Throughout the year Samba schools have been working in fierce competition creating original music and dance on the carnival theme. The festivities are so widespread that shops, businesses and government offices all close while the carnival lasts.

Brazil also has its own passion play which started in 1950 at the village of Fazenda Nova. Every year a large cast of volunteers acts out Christ's arrest, trial and execution. They are watched by an audience of thousands.

## Freeing the prisoners

In the town of Popayan, Colombia, another event in the Easter story is remembered through the annual Feast of Prisoners. Church and government representatives make a procession to the local prison accompanied by the army band and children.

All the prisoners are treated to a ceremonial banquet, after which one prisoner is chosen, given food and money and set free at the end of the day. The custom is based on the time when Pontius Pilate released the prisoner Barabbas at the crowd's request rather than freeing Jesus.

Easter ceremonies have been held in the town since 1558. Once even a war was held up so that the celebrations could go ahead. For the Colombians it was a fitting reminder that all Easter parades are descended from the very first Palm Sunday when the King of Peace was welcomed into Jerusalem.

# AN EASTER TABLE

An essential part of every festival is decorating the house. Easter is no exception. Just as Christmas wouldn't be the same without a decorated tree, in some countries the Easter tree, hung with painted eggs or dough figures, is still the focal point.

In Sweden the Easter tree is made from birch branches and arranged in a vase, while in Germany it is made from a cross shape of wooden rods covered in greenery. In Holland a popular Palm Sunday custom is for children to carry their palm crosses in procession. On the top of each cross perches an Easter cockerel made from dough.

**Here are several ideas for decorating a traditional Easter table.**

### EASTER TREE

◇ A simple Easter tree can be made from a branch of twigs sprayed silver or gold.
◇ Hang decorated eggs from ribbons on the branches. For a quick and simple effect, spray eggs with bright paints. More elaborate methods of egg decorating are on page 79–81.
◇ Make dough shapes to hang on your Easter tree. Some traditional ideas are a rising sun (symbol of Jesus rising to life), a cockerel (the awakener to the new day) or a man and woman to represent the human race Jesus came to save. Use the dough recipe for hot cross buns (page 69) and roll it out to a thickness of ½ inch. Cut out the figures. Add currants for the eyes. Leave to rise in a warm place for half an hour then bake until golden brown. When done, glaze with golden syrup.

### NEST EGGS

**These nest eggs make fun decorations which children can display on the Easter table and present to their friends as gifts.**

#### You need:

◇ ¼ cup butter or margarine
◇ 2 tbsp light corn syrup
◇ 4 tbsp drinking chocolate or cocoa powder
◇ 12 tbsp cornflakes or rice cereal
◇ Paper muffin-cases
◇ Chocolate or sugar coated mini-eggs

#### To make:

1 Melt the butter or margarine into a saucepan together with the syrup.

2 Stir in the drinking chocolate or cocoa powder. Add in the cereal and mix together well.

3 Spoon the mixture into the paper muffin-cases. Press a hollow into the middle of the mixture to make a nest.

4 When set, fill each nest with chocolate or sugar coated mini-eggs.

# BLOOMING BOWL

A vase of flowers always makes a beautiful decoration. If you want flowers that will last the whole of Easter, try this bright bunch of daffodils. Children can make them with a little adult help.

## You need:

◇ 5 pieces of card 4 x 4in.
◇ Yellow paint
◇ An egg carton
◇ Glue
◇ 5 'bendable' drinking straws

## To make:

1 Cut out five flower shapes from the card and paint yellow on both sides.

2 Cut out five cups from the egg carton and paint yellow.

3 Glue the bottom of the cups onto the middle of each flower.

4 Paint the drinking straws in green paint and leave them to dry.

5 Make a small hole with scissors in the back of each flower. Push a drinking straw through and bend the end over so that it stays in place.

# EASTER GAMES FOR CHILDREN

Easter is a time when many children are on holiday from school. If you're running short of things to do, here are some ideas for games and activities on an Easter theme. They are ideal for an Easter children's party.

## Wobbling bunnies

A game which younger children will enjoy. Players must pretend to be bunnies by hopping around in a crouching position. When you shout 'Hunter's coming!' everyone must stop and keep completely still without wobbling. After a few seconds shout 'Hunter's gone!' and they can continue hopping around. After a few practice rounds, any player that wobbles must drop out until only the winner is left.

## Egg and spoon

A traditional outdoor race which is great fun. Each player balances a hard-boiled egg on a wooden spoon. They must race to the winning line holding their egg and spoon in one hand. If the egg falls off they can only continue once the egg is back on the spoon. If you prefer, use small chocolate Easter eggs instead of real ones.

## Easter bonnets

In parts of Britain and in the United States , it used to be traditional to wear a new bonnet for Easter. One way of keeping younger children amused is to give them an old hat and bits of material such as ribbon, beads, plastic flowers, feathers etc. See who can make the best Easter bonnet and have a parade to show off the results.

## Egg painting

A similar pastime to Easter bonnets. You'll need several hard-boiled eggs, poster paints, glue and festive materials such as ribbon, braid or lace. Give each child an egg and ask them to decorate it. If the children are older, you could add an element of excitement by giving them a time limit in which to finish (say 10 minutes).

## Tail on the donkey

The donkey which Jesus rode on Palm Sunday is the hero of this much-loved game. Draw a simple picture of a tail-less donkey and pin it to a blackboard or piece of thick cardboard. Cut out a tail from card and put a large pin through the top. Children take turns pinning the tail on the donkey while blindfolded. Mark each child's attempt with their initials (even if it ends up on an ear or a nose!) The one who puts the tail in the right place (or who is nearest) is the winner.

## Egg Hunt

The ideal end to any Easter party or gathering is an Easter egg hunt. Chocolate or sugar coated mini-eggs can be hidden around the garden under trees, plants or rocks. Children of all ages cannot resist the hunt to find them.

# *A* *Taste of Easter*

*While they were eating, Jesus took a piece of bread, gave*
*a prayer of thanks, broke it and gave it to his disciples.*

**The Gospel of Mark**

**While Lent has traditionally been kept as a time for fasting—
giving up some sorts of food—the Easter festival that follows is
a time for feasting. Foods that have a special place on the Easter
table include several kinds of bread, buns and pretzels, roast
lamb, eggs, pies and a variety of delicious cakes.**

**Food also plays a central role in the Jewish festival of
Passover. It was the Passover meal that Jesus shared with his
disciples on the night he was betrayed by Judas into the hands
of the Jewish authorities. We now call that meal the Last
Supper. Jesus' disciple John was one of the people there.**

## John's story

Even the way we found the room was
strange. Jesus sent Peter and me on ahead.
We were to look for a man carrying a jar of
water and follow him to the house he
entered. We found him just as Jesus had
said and asked him about a room where we
could eat our Passover meal. He merely
nodded as if he'd been expecting us earlier
and showed us upstairs to a large furnished
room.

When the others arrived there was a kind
of tension between us. No one spoke too
much—we were all waiting to see what Jesus
would do. Everyone had heard that the
priests and elders were plotting to have him
arrested; we ate the meal with a feeling that
someone might come and break down the
door at any minute.

What Jesus said to us did nothing to set
my mind at rest. When he had thanked God
for the bread as usual he broke it in pieces
saying, 'Take this and eat it, this is my
body.' And the same thing with the wine—
something about it being his blood poured

# JUDAS

Not many people would name a child Judas today, for the name has come to mean a betrayer.

The measure of Judas Iscariot's betrayal is that he was one of Jesus' closest companions—a member of the twelve disciples and keeper of the purse (which we're told he stole from).

So what was Judas' motive for betraying Jesus? Several reasons have been suggested: disappointment—at Jesus' failure to lead a rebellion against the Romans; greed—for the money offered as bounty on Jesus' head; or fear—at the likely consequences of Jesus' actions, which persuaded him to try to save his own skin.

The Bible doesn't spell out Judas' motives for betrayal; but it does record that it did him no good; he died soon afterwards, either by accident or suicide.

out for us. I'm not sure any of us understood what he meant at the time—it was only afterwards we remembered his words.

Then, while the meal was still only half over, he looked at all of us and said, 'One of you will betray me.'

A chill passed over the room. No one was eating or drinking now. Our eyes travelled around the table from one face to another.

One by one we found our voices and began to protest, 'Surely not me? You can't mean me!'

Jesus didn't answer. He leaned forward and dipped a piece of bread in the bowl. 'One of you who dips his bread in the dish with me will betray me.'

It was then that Judas left. He'd been protesting his innocence like the rest of us but then he quietly withdrew from the circle and slipped out of the door. Some said Jesus had told him to go and buy something else for the festival since he was the one in charge of the money bag. Only afterwards did we understand the business he'd gone on. It was a matter not of buying but of selling—thirty pieces of silver in exchange for Jesus' life.

# THE PASSOVER MEAL

The word for Easter in many European languages is *Pasch*, a Greek term that comes from the Hebrew Passover. The Passover is a celebratory meal which was first held thousands of years ago and is still eaten every year in Orthodox Jewish households.

The Passover meal is a reminder of a turning-point in Jewish history, recorded in the Old Testament book of Exodus, when the nation of Israel was delivered from slavery in Egypt. On that night God struck the firstborn Egyptians with death but 'passed over' the Israelite households. After that, the king of Egypt let the slaves go free. The Passover feast was to remind generations of Jewish families how God had rescued them from captivity and protected them.

Today the Passover meal follows a traditional pattern. First the cup of wine is blessed—the first of four cups of wine that are shared during the meal. Then each person takes a handful of herbs which they dip in salt water. The herbs signify the suffering of the Israelites during their slavery in Egypt.

Next comes the unleavened bread. It was made without yeast so that it could not spoil on the journey. The head of the household breaks a cake of bread and puts some aside. The youngest member of the household then asks the questions which can only be answered by telling the story of the first Passover, beginning:

'Why is this night different from all other nights and why do we eat unleavened bread?'

After the story has been heard, psalms are sung and the second cup of wine is passed round.

Before the meal itself proceeds, everyone washes their hands, God is thanked for the food, and the bread is broken. The bitter herb dipped in sauce is distributed and then it is time for the main dish of the meal. Roast lamb is eaten because, on the night before their flight from Egypt, each Israelite family killed a lamb, ate the meat and daubed the blood over their doorway as a sign of God's protection.

After the lamb, the bread laid aside earlier is eaten and the third cup of wine is passed from person to person. Finally the ceremony ends with the singing of psalms known as the *Hallel* (hallelujah) psalms, praising God.

Jesus would have eaten a meal much like this in the upper room the night before his crucifixion. But his words gave the ceremony a completely new meaning. Just as Israel received God's protection through the sacrifice of a lamb, Jesus, whom John the Baptist had called the Lamb of God, was about to offer his life to bring freedom for the whole world.

# FOOD FOR PASSOVER

Today, the meal in the Upper Room has become part of Holy Week celebrations for some churches in America. Each of the ingredients in a Passover meal has a special significance:

◇ Three whole matzos (unleavened bread). A piece of the middle one is hidden for a child to find.

◇ A roasted lamb bone—placed to the host's right—in memory of the lamb sacrificed by Israelites the night before their flight from Egypt.

◇ A roasted egg—to the left—in mourning for the destroyed temple.

◇ *Maror* (bitter herbs)—placed in the middle as a reminder of the bitterness of slavery in Egypt.

◇ *Charoseth* (chopped almonds, apple, wine, sugar and cinnamon)—this symbolizes the mortar which the Jews had to mix in making bricks for the king of Egypt.

◇ Salt water—to signify the Red Sea which miraculously parted to let the Israelites across.

◇ *Karpar* (celery, parsley, greens)—the Hebrew word means 600,000, the recorded number who left Egypt.

◇ Elijah's cup—usually a treasured one filled with wine—is placed on the table to await the arrival of the Messiah.

# THE MEAL THAT JESUS GAVE US

*While they were eating, Jesus took a piece of bread, gave a prayer of thanks, broke it and gave it to his disciples. 'Take and eat it,' he said; 'this is my body.' Then he took a cup, gave thanks to God, and gave it to them. 'Drink it all of you,' he said; 'this is my blood which seals God's covenant, my blood poured out for many for the forgiveness of sins.'*
**Matthew's Gospel**

The Passover meal that Jesus shared with his close friends would have been one that was both familiar and new to them. Familiar, in that it kept to the traditional food and pattern of the Jewish Passover, but new in the meaning which Jesus gave parts of the ceremony. Jesus had turned the Passover ritual into a meal that his followers could eat in his memory, reminding them of the reasons why he died.

Before the meal, Jesus did something which amazed his disciples. He wrapped a towel round his waist and washed the feet of each person present. This menial task was normally left to a servant. By it Jesus was showing how he wanted his followers to love one another. The message was clear: if their master and Lord could wash their feet then no act of service was beneath his followers.

Later, when Jesus passed round the broken bread and the cup of wine, he spoke of them as his body and blood. The disciples would have been familar with the significance of bread and wine in the Passover meal, but now Jesus was teaching them something new. Whenever they broke the bread they were to remember how Jesus' body had been broken for them on the cross. When they drank the wine it was to remind them how his blood had been shed to bring forgiveness and reconciliation with God to everyone.

Today the meal that Jesus gave us is known by a variety of names—Communion, Eucharist, Mass and the Lord's Supper are some of them. It is a custom which is full of meaning for all Christians. Not only does it remind them of what Jesus has done in the past, it also speaks of the future when he will return to share 'the wedding feast of the Lamb' with his people at the end of time.

# MAUNDY THURSDAY

The day on which Christians remember the Last Supper is sometimes known as Maundy Thursday. The word *Maundy* probably comes from the Latin word *maundatum* (command) and recalls Christ's words at the Last Supper: 'And now I give you a new commandment: love one another. As I have loved you, so you must love one another.'

The example Jesus set in washing his disciples' feet has sometimes been followed literally in history as a good way of reminding rulers that they are there to serve their subjects.

In England, the custom was preserved until 1689 that the king or queen should wash the feet of the poor every Maundy Thursday in Westminster Abbey. To safeguard the royal nose, the feet were first washed by the Yeoman of the Laundry before the monarch had to cleanse and kiss them.

Food and clothing were also given to the poor. In 1572 Elizabeth I gave each person enough broadcloth for a gown and a pair of sleeves, half a side of salmon, six red herrings, bread and claret. By the reign of Queen Victoria the presents had changed to woollen and linen clothing, shoes and stockings to the men, and 35 shillings to the women.

Today the custom is still observed but the foot washing has sadly disappeared and the gift of clothing has been replaced by specially minted Maundy money. A Yeoman of the Guard carries a golden tray on which

the white leather purses containing the coins are displayed. The Queen (or whoever is performing the ceremony) carries a nosegay of flowers—a traditional protection at the time of the Great Plague. The clergy have linen towels on their shoulders as the sole reminder of the footwashing days.

England is not the only country to observe this custom. In former times Austrian Emperors were called on to wash the feet of twelve old men and give them a splendid banquet. The footwashing tradition is also continued in Eastern Orthodox and Catholic churches. In Rome, the Pope washes the feet of thirteen priests at a ceremony in St Peter's Basilica.

# EASTER FEASTS

Almost every country has its own special Easter recipes. In Russia you might be treated to *Kulich*, an Easter bread, or *Pasha*, a sort of cheesecake. The Swedes eat Fat Tuesday buns while the British feast on hot cross buns. Lamb will probably feature on most Easter tables—certainly in Greece, where it may be served stuffed with almonds and raisins. There are far too many recipes to include them all, but here is a selection to give you a taste of Easter around the world.

## STARTERS AND MAIN COURSES

### BORSCHT (RUSSIA)

If you've gorged too many Easter eggs or need a starter to your Easter meal then this colorful Russian soup may be just the thing. Serve it hot or chilled.

#### Ingredients:

◇ 1 small potato
◇ 1lb raw beetroot
◇ 1 medium onion
◇ 2 tbsp butter or margarine
◇ 4 cups vegetable stock
◇ 3 tbsp cider vinegar
◇ 1 tsp yeast extract
◇ Ground nutmeg
◇ Salt and pepper
◇ Sour cream and chopped parsley to garnish

#### To make:

1  Wash and chop the vegetables.

2  Melt the butter and sauté the onion until transparent.

3  Add the potato, beetroot and stock. Bring to the boil.

4  Reduce the heat. Cover and simmer for 30 minutes.

5  Allow to cool. Blend in small amounts, using a blender or food processor.

6  Return to pan. Add vinegar, yeast extract, nutmeg and seasoning.

7  Reheat to serving temperature or cover and chill until required.

8  Stir in a swirl of sour cream and sprinkle with parsley just before serving.

## LAMB WITH ORANGE SAUCE
## (ENGLAND)

Lamb cutlets make a succulent dish when served with a light citrus sauce.

### Ingredients:

◇ 1 tbsp butter or margarine
◇ 1 tbsp oil
◇ 1 clove garlic
◇ 8 lamb cutlets
◇ Juice of 1 orange
◇ 2 tsp corn starch
◇ 1/2 cup lamb stock
◇ 2 tsp soft brown sugar
◇ 2 tbsp chopped watercress
◇ Salt and pepper
◇ Watercress and orange slices to garnish

### To make:

1  Heat the butter and oil in a large frying pan. Crush the garlic and fry gently in the oil without browning. Remove from the pan with a slotted spoon.

2  Add the cutlets to the garlic-flavored oil, and fry for 4–5 minutes on each side. Remove from the pan and keep warm.

3  Blend the orange juice with the corn starch and stir into the juices left in the pan along with the stock and sugar. Bring to the boil. Add the chopped watercress and seasoning and simmer for a minute or until the sauce begins to thicken.

4  Pour the sauce over the cutlets and garnish with the orange slices and sprigs of watercress. Serve with fresh vegetables and potatoes.

## EASTER CHICKEN CASSEROLE
## (DENMARK)

This favorite Danish recipe uses chicken and mushrooms covered with a lattice of egg strips

### Ingredients:

◇ 4 chicken pieces
◇ 6 small onions
◇ 4 tbsp butter
◇ 2 tbsp chopped parsley
◇ 2 cups chicken stock
◇ 8oz mushrooms, sliced
◇ Salt and pepper
◇ 8oz frozen peas
◇ 2 eggs
◇ 2 tbsp milk
◇ 2 tbsp corn starch

### To make:

1  Fry the chicken pieces in butter with the onions until they're lightly browned. Add the stock, the sliced mushrooms, seasoning and a tablespoon of parsley.

2  Simmer for half an hour in a covered saucepan, adding the peas for the final ten minutes.

3  Beat the eggs and milk together with a little seasoning. Melt a knob of butter in a frying pan and cook the mixture until firm.

4  Drain off the stock and thicken it with corn starch blended with a little water. Pour the gravy over the chicken.

5  Cut the egg into strips and criss-cross it over the chicken. Garnish with the remaining parsley.

## SPANA KOPITTA—SPINACH AND CHEESE PIE (GREECE)

**If you want a vegetarian option for the Easter table, this Greek dish offers a mouthwatering combination of spinach and feta cheese wrapped in delicate filo pastry.**

### Ingredients:

◇ 1 bunch scallions, chopped
◇ 1¹/₂ sticks butter
◇ 2 eggs
◇ 2lb spinach, washed and drained
◇ 8oz feta cheese, crumbled
◇ 8oz ready-made filo pastry
◇ 8oz cottage cheese
◇ 2 tbsp corn starch
◇ 2 tbsp chopped fresh parsley
◇ 2 tbsp chopped fresh dill
◇ Salt and pepper to taste

### To make:

1 Preheat the oven to 375°F. Sauté the onions in a third of the butter until tender.

2 Chop the spinach and cook in a large covered pan with a little water until wilted. Drain, pressing out as much moisture as possible.

3 Mix together onions, eggs, feta, cottage cheese, corn starch, herbs and spinach. Season lightly.

4 Butter an oblong dish approximately 12 x 9in.

5 Place filo pastry under a damp cloth. Remove one sheet, brush with melted butter and line the dish. Repeat with five sheets, brushing each one with melted butter.

6 Spread the spinach and cheese filling over the pastry.

7 Cover with the remaining sheets of pastry, brushing with melted butter as before.

8 Reduce oven heat to 350°F. Bake for 50 minutes until golden brown and puffed.

9 Allow to stand for 5–15 minutes before serving.

# EASTER BREADS AND DESSERTS

## FOLAR (PORTUGAL)

**Folar is a popular Easter bread in Portugal, made from sweet dough and often decorated with eggs.**

### Ingredients:

◇ 3 sticks melted butter
◇ 2$^{1}/_{3}$ cups evaporated milk
◇ 4oz yeast
◇ 1$^{1}/_{2}$ cups sugar
◇ 4$^{1}/_{2}$ cups flour
◇ 2 cups of water
◇ Lemon juice
◇ Pinch of salt
◇ 2 hard-boiled eggs—plain or colored

1  Preheat oven to 250°F. Mix together milk, melted butter and yeast. Add water and beat.

2  Add sugar, salt and lemon juice, stir well.

3  Mix in the flour to form a dough.

4  Knead well on a floured surface until the dough is smooth.

5  Cover dough with greased clear food wrap. Leave to rise for 45–60 minutes.

6  Divide the dough into 3 equal parts and form them into 3 long sausage shapes.

7  Plait these together and then join the ends to form a round plait.

8  Allow the plait to stand on a greased and floured baking sheet for 30 minutes.

9  Make two wells in the plait and put in two hard-boiled eggs, colored beforehand if desired.

10 Place in pre-heated oven and cook for one hour.

## PASHA—EASTER CHEESECAKE (RUSSIA)

**Pasha has been a traditional rich Easter dessert in Russia for generations. It should be made the night before eating.**

### Ingredients:

◇ 4 tbsp butter or margarine
◇ $^{1}/_{4}$ cup sugar
◇ 1 egg yolk
◇ 1lb cottage cheese
◇ 1 tsp vanilla extract
◇ 4 tbsp sour cream
◇ $^{1}/_{3}$ cup chopped almonds
◇ $^{1}/_{3}$ cup mixed glacé fruit
◇ $^{3}/_{4}$ cup whipping cream
◇ Glacé cherries

### To make:

1  Beat butter and sugar in a large bowl until fluffy, using an electric mixer.

2  Beat in egg yolk, cottage cheese, sour cream, almonds, fruit and vanilla until smooth and well blended.

3  Whip and then carefully fold in $^{2}/_{3}$ cup of the whipped cream.

4  Place mixture in a greased bowl and refrigerate overnight.

5  Just before eating, turn cheesecake out onto a serving dish and decorate with the remaining whipped cream and the glacé cherries.

## CASSATA ALLA SICILIANA (ITALY)

**A magnificent madeira cake layered with ricotta cheese and fruit filling. It is best served on the same day it is made.**

### Ingredients:

**Cake**
◇ 1³/₄ sticks softened butter
◇ 1 cup sugar
◇ 4 eggs
◇ 2 cups flour
◇ 1 tbsp baking powder
◇ 4 tbsp sherry or milk

**Filling and coating**
◇ 1³/₄ cups ricotta cheese
◇ ¹/₂ cup sugar
◇ 2 tbsp maraschino liqueur (if desired)
◇ ¹/₂ cup glacé cherries, chopped
◇ ¹/₄ oz angelica, finely chopped
◇ ¹/₃ cup dried apricots, chopped
◇ ¹/₃ cup raisins
◇ Finely grated zest of ¹/₂ lemon
◇ ³/₄ cup chopped almonds, toasted
◇ 4 tbsp apricot jam, melted and sieved

### To make the cake:

1 Heat the oven to 325° F. Grease and line a loaf tin 9 x 5 x 3in.

2 Beat the butter and sugar together until light and creamy.

3 Beat in the eggs, one at a time.

4 Sift together the flour and baking powder and stir into the cake mixture.

5 Add the sherry or milk and mix in well.

6 Turn the mixture into the prepared loaf tin and level the top.

7 Bake for one hour or until the cake is golden , well risen and beginning to come away from the sides of the tin. To test, insert a fine skewer into the center—it should come out clean.

8 Allow the cake to cool for while before turning out onto a wire rack. Leave to get cold.

### To add the filling:

9 Beat the ricotta cheese with the sugar until fluffy and stiff. Mix in the liqueur, fruits and lemon zest.

10 Slice the cold cake horizontally into four layers, then sandwich the ricotta filling between them. Press down lightly.

11 Put the toasted almonds on a sheet of waxed paper. Brush the sides of the cake with the warm, melted jam. Holding the cake by top and bottom, dip it into the toasted almonds. Brush the top of the cake with jam and sprinkle on more almonds.

12 Serve cut into thick slices on a plate.

## CHOCOLATE EASTER NEST

**A tempting nest of mini Easter eggs that will delight children and chocaholics!**

### Ingredients:

**Cake**
◇ 1 stick soft margarine
◇ $1/2$ cup sugar
◇ $3/4$ cup light corn syrup
◇ $1/4$ cup flaked coconut
◇ $1/4$ cup cocoa powder, sieved
◇ 1 cup self-rising flour, sieved
◇ 3 tbsp milk
◇ 2 eggs, beaten

**Icing and decoration**
◇ 6 tbsp butter or margarine
◇ 1 cup powdered sugar, sieved
◇ 1 tbsp cocoa powder
◇ 2 tbsp hot water
◇ 1 tbsp milk
◇ $1/4$ cup flaked coconut, toasted
◇ Mini chocolate eggs or sugared almonds

### To make the cake:

1  Preheat the oven to 350°F.

2  Grease an 8in. ring mold and dust with sugar.

3  Cream the margarine and sugar until light and fluffy. Beat in the syrup.

4  Add the coconut, sieved cocoa, flour, milk and eggs. Beat well and spoon into the prepared tin, levelling the surface.

5  Bake for 45 minutes in the middle of the oven. Insert a fine skewer into the center—it should come out clean.

6  Leave for 5 minutes before turning out onto a wire rack to cool.

### To make the icing:

7  Put the butter in a bowl with the powdered sugar.

8  Blend the cocoa with the hot water and add with the milk. Beat well and spread over the cake evenly.

9  To decorate, sprinkle the top with the toasted coconut and fill the center with brightly wrapped mini Easter eggs or sugared almonds.

# *T*he Passion Story

*Then Jesus said to them, 'This very night all of you will turn away and leave me.'*
*Peter spoke up and said to Jesus, 'I will never leave you, even though all the rest do!'*
*Jesus said to Peter, 'I tell you that before the cock crows tonight, you will say three times that you do not know me.'*

**The Gospel of Matthew**

**The events of Jesus' last days are sometimes known as the Passion story. The Passion refers to Jesus' suffering in his betrayal, arrest, trial, and death on the cross. It begins in the darkness of the Garden of Gethsemane where Jesus often went with his friends. One of them was Peter, who had promised never to leave Jesus.**

## Peter's story

'Not me. They may all run away and leave you but not me. Never.' My own words came back to taunt me, hissing with the damp twigs on the fire.

We had gone to Gethsemane after the meal. It was a secret place Jesus often took us to when he wanted to be away from the crowds. But this night he was troubled. He said he wanted to pray, asking James, John and me to keep him company.

The three of us sat down under the olive trees while he went a little further on.

I remember watching the moon drift slowly between the clouds and thinking that I mustn't let my eyes close. Jesus was kneeling and whispering something, 'Father, if it is possible, take this cup away from me . . .'

Later when he woke me there were lights coming towards us. Twenty or more torches moving through the dark in our direction. I glanced at James and John. It was too late to run and Jesus showed no sign of moving. As the crowd drew closer we saw they were

guards with spears, backed by a rabble armed with clubs and sticks.

Judas was at the front. He stepped forward to greet Jesus, kissing him on the cheek. It was the signal they'd been waiting for. The soldiers moved in fast to seize Jesus. I drew the sword I had with me and lashed out at one of the mob, catching him on the ear. But Jesus called to me to put my sword away. Four men were holding him, pinning his arms on each side. I looked around for help from the others; most of them had gone, vanished like ghosts in the night.

But not me. I followed at a distance, with John. They took Jesus to the house of the high priest, Caiaphas. John spoke to the girl on the door and got us in as far as the courtyards where a number of servants and officials were warming themselves around a fire.

I squeezed in among them hoping to hear something about Jesus. I pulled my cloak up higher to try and hide my face, but a servant girl had been watching me.

'That's one of them there,' she said. 'One of his Galilean friends.'

'I don't know him,' I replied quickly. Unluckily I recognized one of the mob from the olive grove standing around the fire. Before long he was accusing me too: 'I know you, you were with him!' But again I swore furiously that he was wrong.

'Yes, you're a Galilean too, I can tell from your accent,' another started in.

'I'm not! I don't know what you're talking about,' I shouted, ready to seize him by the throat. But my words died away. A cock was crowing in the courtyard. Jesus' words came back to me: 'Before the cock crows today, you will disown me three times.'

'Not me. Never,' I'd said. The words returned to taunt me, hissing with the damp twigs on the fire.

# PETER THE HOTHEAD

Of all Jesus' disciples, Peter is the one whom the Gospels paint most vividly. Every group has a hothead—the one who usually speaks up first and loudest, who leaps into action while others are still calculating the odds. Peter was such a character, earning the nickname 'the rock' from Jesus because of his strength and loyalty. He was a fisherman from the lakeside town of Bethsaida in Galilee, who heard of Jesus through his brother Andrew.

Peter and Andrew were among the twelve disciples who spent three years with Jesus, observing him, learning from him and taking part in his mission. When, near the end of that period, Jesus asked his disciples, 'Who do you say I am?' it was Peter who spoke up with typical bluntness: 'You are the Christ, the Son of the living God.'

Peter's denial of Jesus in the courtyard was a failure from which he might never have recovered. His cowardice cost him bitter tears. But after the resurrection, Jesus restored Peter to the leadership of the disciples by asking him three times, 'Do you love me?' This time Peter passed the test and went on to play a central role in the building of the early Christian church.

# OBERAMMERGAU — THE PLAY TO KEEP A PROMISE

Before books were printed—and before most of the population could read—ordinary people learned about the world by listening to stories. Christians consider the Easter story to be the greatest of all time, so it is not surprising that different ways were found to pass it on to each new generation. One method was the passion play, a dramatic enactment of the events of the Passion story often performed on Good Friday. Since early times, Passion plays have been performed in town squares, halls and churches all over Europe, but none is more famous than that of Oberammergau.

## A plague and a promise

In 1633 the Black Death was sweeping Europe, and the people of Oberammergau, a village in Austria, feared for its safety. When the plague came to an end, the villagers made a vow as an expression of their gratitude to God. Their vow was that every ten years they would perform a Passion play. Over 350 years later, the promise has been kept faithfully. Today the Oberammergau Passion Play is so famous throughout the world that it has to be performed in a huge open-air theatre with seating for 5,000 people.

Only those families who have lived in the village for twenty years or more are allowed to take part. The cast includes two hundred children and 123 speaking parts, which are a matter of intense rivalry. Women have been known to postpone their marriages for the play since only single females under thirty-five are eligible to play a part. A selection committee headed by the *Burgermeister* and the parish priest has the difficult responsibilty of choosing who will play the leading roles.

Rehearsals for the play start about two years in advance. Most of the cast are also tradespeople—postmen, shopkeepers, hotel managers and craftsmen. There is an abundance of woodcarvers since the village is also famous for its crafts, especially beautifully carved nativity scenes.

Despite the play's international renown, it has managed to resist the temptation of commercialization. The actors are only paid what they have lost from their normal earnings to be in the play. Villagers have steadfastly refused to take the play beyond Oberammergau—even Hollywood was shown the door when it suggested a film version.

No make-up is worn; the men are expected to grow real beards for the performance (apart from Pontius Pilate who, as a Roman, is allowed to go clean shaven). Real animals are also used, including sheep and donkeys. In the scene where Jesus overturns the tables of the moneychangers in the temple, white doves escape and fly out from their cages. Fortunately they return for the next performance as they are really homing pigeons.

## More than a play

The villagers do not see their performance merely as a dramatic spectacle. They are presenting an act of worship as they retell the timeless events of the Easter story. As one villager put it: 'The Oberammergauer does not feel as if he were acting in a theatre; to us the play means keeping the sacred vow of our forefathers.'

One famous spectator was the writer, Hans Christian Anderson who declared: 'Never shall I forget the Passion Play at Oberammergau, so completely did it surpass all my expectation ... The whole religious play has a majesty, a simplicity, something so strangely absorbing that even the most irreligious must needs be dumb.'

# JESUS CHRIST
# MOVIE STAR

## Q. Which two characters in history have had most films made about them?
## A. Napoleon and Jesus Christ.

While it is easy to see what attracted movie makers to the epic battle-torn life of the French Emperor, Jesus has always presented more of a problem to directors and screenwriters. To begin with, he doesn't fit into the mold of the conventional Hollywood hero who spends most of his time in fights or embraces. He is also both man and God, a challenge which prompted one actor to say: 'Nobody can play Christ.'

The earliest attempts to capture the Gospel stories on celluloid were black and white silent films, melodramatic by today's standards. These were soon overtaken by the 1927 epic *King of Kings*, the most

expensive silent movie ever made. Its producer, Cecil B. De Mille, was less interested in historical accuracy than lavish spectacle—which may explain why Mary Magdalene appears in the film as a fabulously wealthy courtesan in love with Judas. De Mille can claim to have discovered the biblical epic, and he went on to exploit its possibilities shamelessly in films such as *Ben Hur*, *The Robe* and *The Ten Commandments*.

In Britain, the new Board of Censors was getting uneasy about Christ appearing in films and sought to ban the practice. This led to bizarre films such as *Barabbas* (1935), which featured a Jesus who can be heard but not seen.

By the 1960s ideas had changed and George Stevens was able to cast Max Von Sydow as Jesus in the most expensive attempt at the story yet. *The Greatest Story Ever Told* boasted a budget of millions and a star-studded supporting cast. John Wayne as the centurion is remembered for drawling the immortal line: 'Surely this man was the

Son of Gahd.' Nevertheless the film was a box-office flop and discouraged Hollywood from risking big money on the story again.

Meanwhile in Europe, a low-budget life of Jesus was causing a sensation. Passolini's *The Gospel According to St Matthew* shocked many by depicting a Christ who smouldered with the anger and passion of a revolutionary. The unknown Spanish student who played the lead was later punished for taking part in 'Communist propaganda'.

By the late sixties and early seventies, the hippie generation was claiming Jesus as one of its own. The screen versions of *Godspell* and *Jesus Christ Superstar* portray Jesus as a shock-headed clown and as an early rock star.

Other attempts to capture Jesus on celluloid have followed, some popular, such as Zefferelli's *Jesus of Nazareth* and some controversial, such as *The Last Temptation of Christ*.

For a hundred years the movies have been selling Jesus as a hero of many faces—the meek and mild Sunday school Jesus, the revolutionary Jesus, the actor/singer Jesus. Each film chooses its own personal view of Christ, with a nod to history but inevitably influenced by the thinking of its own generation.

Perhaps the actor Robert Powell was right in saying, 'Nobody can play Christ', since how can any actor hope to convey someone who is both man and God at the same time? Films will no doubt go on trying to present new faces of Jesus for many years to come, but—just as certainly—the real Jesus will survive them all.

# TREMBLE AND THUNDER

## AN EASTER PLAY FOR CHILDREN

This original play can be performed by children with a little help from an adult. The story can be used either as a puppet play or as drama in schools, churches and children's clubs, or simply for a few children who enjoy story-telling.

If there are only a small number (2–5 children) involved, the script can be used for a puppet play, with one or more children reading the story. Simple instructions for making the finger puppets can be found on page 53.

If you have six or more children who would like to take part, the story can be acted out as a play. You will need to create some animal masks for Tremble and Thunder out of strong card and elastic. Other characters can wear easy-to-make tunic style costumes cut out of sheets or striped material.

# THE CAST

Narrator—Naomi

Tremble the donkey

Thunder the horse

Peter and John—Jesus' friends

Jesus

Townspeople (as many as you want)

*(Enter Naomi),*

**Naomi:** Hello, my name is Naomi. My family lives in a little white house at the edge of Jerusalem. At the back of my house is a field where we keep two animals. One of them I call Thunder.

*(Enter Thunder who walks proudly up and down)*

**Naomi:** Thunder is a very old horse. I think she once belonged to someone important, but my father only uses her to pull the plow. Our other animal is a young donkey.

*(Enter Tremble shyly)*

**Naomi:** I call him Tremble because every time anyone goes near him, he starts to tremble.

*(Naomi approaches him and Tremble starts to tremble)*

**Naomi:** See what I mean? Sometimes when I've got nothing to do I lean over the fence and watch Thunder and Tremble together. You would almost think they were talking to each other.

**Tremble** *(eating)*: Mmm, this grass tastes very sweet today.

**Thunder:** Not as sweet as the hay I used to eat in the king's stables. Did I ever tell you about the days when I belonged to the king?

**Tremble** *(wearily)*: Yes, I think you did, Thunder.

**Thunder:** When I belonged to the king I ate the best oats and hay every mealtime. And the king's servant would brush my coat every morning.

**Tremble:** How wonderful!

**Thunder:** And if there was a battle, the king commanded, 'Saddle up Thunder!' And they'd bring the red saddle with the gold tassels. And the king would ride me into battle with my hooves drumming and my mane flying in the wind.

**Tremble** *(beginning to tremble)*: Please don't talk about battles.

**Thunder:** The king's sword would go swish, swish and he'd kill all his enemies.

**Tremble:** Stop, you're making me tremble! Nobody has ever ridden on my back.

**Thunder:** Of course not! Who'd want to ride a wobbly little donkey who goes all trembly when anyone even talks to him?

**Naomi:** Poor Tremble! He always looked so worried. Anyway, the day I want to tell you about, I was leaning over my fence as usual when two men came to see me.

*(Enter Peter and John. They approach Naomi)*

**Peter:** Morning! It's a fine morning.

**Naomi:** Yes, it is. What can I do for you?

**John:** Are those your animals in the field?

**Naomi:** Yes, they belong to our family. The old horse is Thunder and the young donkey I call Tremble.

**Peter:** We'd like to borrow one of them, if you wouldn't mind.

**Naomi:** Borrow one? What for?

**John:** For something important. Don't worry, we'll bring it straight back.

**Peter:** It's the king who needs it.

**Thunder:** Did you hear that, Tremble? The king needs me! Those must be his servants who have come to fetch me.

**Tremble:** How exciting for you, Thunder!

**Thunder** *(trotting up and down proudly)*: Yes, I knew they'd come back for me one day.

*(Peter and John walk past Thunder and go over to Tremble)*

**Peter:** Come on then, little donkey, we've got a job for you. Oh, poor thing, you're all a tremble.

*(They lead Tremble off)*

**Thunder** *(going after them)*: Hey! You've made a mistake. It's me you want! Me—Thunder!

*(All exit leaving Naomi alone on stage)*

**Naomi:** I must say I was surprised they took poor Tremble. But who was this king who wanted him? Why would he want a poor wobbly-legged donkey? I decided to follow them and find out.

*(She exits)*

*(Enter the crowd with palm branches. They gather on either side of the stage)*

*[If you are doing the puppet play, use Peter and John along with 2 other finger puppets to make the crowd.]*

*(Naomi re-enters)*

**Naomi:** When I reached the city gate I met crowds of people. They were all talking about someone called Jesus who was coming to Jerusalem. People were carrying palm branches and standing on tiptoe to see if Jesus was coming. Then suddenly I saw him turning the corner. He was riding on a donkey. And guess whose donkey it was!

*(Enter Jesus riding on Tremble. They parade through the crowds.)*

**Crowds:** Hooray! Hooray for Jesus! God bless the king who comes in the name of the Lord!

*[A song can be sung at this point while Jesus and Tremble parade through the crowds waving their palm branches.]*

## SONG: HURRAY FOR JESUS!

*Chorus:*
*Hurray for Jesus,*
*Riding to Jerusalem,*
*Riding to the city*
*Up a steep and dusty track.*
*Hurray for Jesus,*
*Riding to Jerusalem,*
*Riding there in triumph*
*On a little donkey's back.*

*Wave palms in the air,*
*Spread your bright cloaks*
*   everywhere*
*And sing, sing, sing.*
*Shout out; This is great.*
*Jesus enters through the gate—*
*Our King.*

*Chorus*

**Sister Oswin**

# Hurray for Jesus

**Chorus**

Hur – ray for Je – sus, Rid –ing to Je – ru – sa – lem,
C   Am   Dm   G

Rid –ing to the ci – ty Up a steep and dus – ty track.
Dm   G7   C   D7   Gdim   G

Hur – ray for Je – sus, Rid –ing to Je – ru – sa – lem,
C   Am   Dm   G

Fine

Rid –ing there in tri –umph On a lit – tle don –key's back.
Dm   Fm6   C   G7   C

**Verse**

1, Wave palms in the air, Spread your bright cloaks ev –ery –where And
Am   Em   Fmaj7   C7

sing, sing, sing. Shout out: This is great.
F   D7   G7   C   G7

D.C.

Je – sus en – ters through the gate Our King.
Ab9   Dm   C   G7   C

51

**Naomi:** You never heard such cheering and shouting. Jesus rode Tremble all the way along the road and everybody followed him shouting and singing praises to God.

*(The parade exits following Jesus)*

**Naomi:** It was nearly dark by the time the two men brought Tremble back to our field.

*(Enter Thunder)*

**Thunder:** Tremble! Where have you been? I've been waiting here for hours!

*(Enter Tremble)*

**Tremble:** Hello, Thunder.

**Thunder:** What happened? I heard the crowds cheering. Was it the king?

**Tremble:** Yes, everyone said he was a king.

**Thunder:** I knew it. And he rode you into battle with your hooves drumming and your mane flying. Oh, it should have been me!

**Tremble:** But he didn't ride me into battle, Thunder. He rode me through the streets and everyone cheered and waved.

**Thunder:** But didn't his sword go swish, swish and kill all his enemies?

**Tremble:** No, he didn't have a sword. He hadn't come to kill anyone. I think he wanted to make people happy.

**Thunder:** A king who doesn't have a sword and doesn't ride into battle? He can't have been a real king at all!

**Tremble:** Well I think he was. And I'll tell you something else— when he rode on my back I stopped trembling. I'll never forget this day. I may only be a wobbly-legged donkey but today I was chosen to carry Jesus, the King of Peace on my back.

**Naomi:** And do you know a funny thing? From that day on whenever anyone went near Tremble . . . he didn't tremble at all!

**THE END**

## FINGER PUPPETS

If you'd like to perform *Tremble and Thunder* as a puppet play, use the simple finger puppets shown above. They are easy to make and come to life when you use your fingers through the two holes to make the puppet stand, walk or run.

### You need:

◇ Strong card—enough for 8 puppets, each 5 x 2in.
◇ Scissors
◇ Pen or pencil
◇ Bright poster paints

### To make:

1  Draw the shape of the finger puppet, using the patterns on this page.

2  Cut two holes for your fingers. Push the sharp point of a pair of scissors through the middle of the hole and then cut round the circle.

3  Draw in the face and clothes on the puppet and then paint with poster paints in bright colors.

## MAKE A PUPPET THEATRE

**A puppet theatre for your play can be easily made from a cardboard box.**

### You need:

◇ A large cardboard box
◇ Scissors
◇ Bright poster paints
◇ A colored cloth

### To make:

1 Cut away the bottom flap of the box so that your hands can come up inside.

2 Now cut away the top half of the front flap leaving the bottom half to cover your hands and a 'tab' in a tree shape at each side of the stage.

3 Paint your theatre in red or gold on the outside. Add a sky and grass on the backcloth and paint the trees on the two front tabs.

4 Place the theatre at the back of a table leaving a gap underneath wide enough for your hands. Drape the cloth over the front of the table so that you cannot be seen by your audience.

# *T*he Shadows Gather

*Jesus stood before the Roman governor, who questioned him. 'Are you the king of the Jews?' he asked.*

**The Gospel of Matthew**

**The story of Jesus' arrest and trial is a sorry tale of corruption and self-interest in high places. Under Jewish law, the accused had to be found guilty by the evidence of two different witnesses. But at the trial, none of the witnesses could agree among themselves.**

**Despite the trumped-up charges, Jesus was found guilty of the blasphemy of calling himself the Son of God. He was then taken to Pontius Pilate, the Roman Governor, since only the Roman authorities had the power to pass the death sentence.**

## Pilate's story

As the Governor I have to be in Jerusalem during Passover. These religious festivals can be dangerous; the city is teeming with visitors, tensions mount, people get over-excited and more often than not it ends in violence.

I had barely finished breakfast that morning when they told me the Jewish priests were outside. They'd brought along a prisoner in chains, another one of the wandering miracle men that this country seems to breed. This one had obviously whipped the chief priests into a high state of panic. They accused him of all kinds of things: inciting revolution, telling the people not to pay their taxes, even claiming to be a king. The man stood calmly in the middle.

'Don't you hear all these charges against you?' I asked him. But he made no answer. I wondered if he had all his senses. I tried again, 'Are you the king of the Jews then?'

'As you say,' he replied.

Further questioning got us nowhere. The man was obviously no fool but he simply wasn't taking part in their game. I guessed

that what was really eating the priests was the fact that this fellow was more popular with the people than they were. I wasn't going to execute an innocent man just to satisfy their vanity.

Luckily I saw a way out. It's a custom at Passover that the Governor releases one prisoner as a gesture of goodwill. We had a man called Barabbas in the cells on a riot and murder charge. I would let the people choose between Barabbas and this Jesus.

I had them both brought outside the courtroom where the people could see them.

'Which one of these two do you want me to set free?' I asked. 'Barabbas!' shouted someone at the front. Others took up the cry, 'Give us Barabbas!'

'Then what do you want me to do with Jesus the Messiah?'

'Crucify him! Crucify him!'

This wasn't what I'd anticipated. The priests were behind it somehow. But the crowd was getting restless, chanting and baying for blood. In my position, there was nothing more I could do. To risk a riot was unthinkable. What if reports should reach the Emperor that I couldn't keep control? Better to wash my hands of the whole affair. I handed Jesus over to be whipped and crucified.

Remember, in this matter I was not responsible. It's these religious festivals. They're dangerous. It always ends in violence.

# THE GOD WHO SUFFERS

The fact that Jesus was arrested, tried, and sentenced on trumped-up charges has been an inspiration throughout history to Christians who have been unjustly imprisoned for their beliefs and actions. The first Christians soon met opposition to their message and the two leading figures in the early church, Peter and Paul, both spent

time in prison for spreading their faith. Far from despairing at the situation, Paul wrote that he saw his chains as a way of helping to spread the message:

*As a result, the whole palace guard and all the others here know that I am in prison because I am a servant of Christ. And my being in prison has given most of the brothers more confidence in the Lord, so that they grow bolder all the time to preach the message fearlessly.*

**Paul's letter to the Philippians**

## John Bunyan

Other Christians have demonstrated that it is impossible to imprison the message of Jesus, even if you lock his followers in the darkest dungeon. If John Bunyan, the seventeenth century Puritan preacher, had not been imprisoned then the world might never have seen his great book, *The Pilgrim's Progress*. The passage which describes Mr Stand-fast at the dark river of death could easily be written of Bunyan himself.

*I see myself now at the end of my journey, my toilsome days are ended. I am going now to see that head that was crowned with thorns, and that face that was spit upon, for me. I have formerly lived by hear-say and faith, but now I go where I shall live by sight, and shall be with him, in whose company I delight myself.*

## Terry Waite

In modern times prisoners have sometimes been used as hostages to bargain for political gain. Terry Waite, the Archbishop of Canterbury's envoy, put his own life at risk on a mission to the Middle East to try to secure the release of Western hostages. Instead, Waite himself was taken hostage and spent 1,763 days alone in a darkened cell, never knowing whether he would see the light of day again. On his return to England, he spoke of a moment which kept his hopes alive during his long ordeal:

*I was kept in total and complete isolation for four years. I saw no one and spoke to no one apart from a cursory word with my guards when they brought my food. And one day out of the blue a guard came with a postcard. It was a postcard showing a stained glass window from Bedford showing John Bunyan in jail . . . And I turned the card over and there was a message from someone I didn't know simply saying: 'We remember; we shall not forget. We shall continue to pray for you and to work for all people who are detained around the world.'*

Jesus warned that many of his followers would face persecution and imprisonment. But he also left them a hope which nothing could take away from them. For even when faced with death, the Christian can say, with John Bunyan, 'Now I go where I shall live by sight, and shall be with him, in whose company I delight myself.'

# PILATE

Pontius Pilate was the fifth Roman Governor of Judea. His powers were far-reaching. He was ruler of the province with the occupying army under his control. He also appointed the high priests and controlled the temple and its funds—a matter of bitter resentment among the Jews.

According to the Jewish historian Josephus, his relationship with his subjects was stormy. He'd first angered them by bringing banners into Jerusalem which bore the Emperor's head, when Jewish law allowed no images that could be worshipped instead of God. Later he had confiscated temple funds and put down riots with ruthless brutality. By the time Jesus arrived on the scene, Pilate knew he couldn't afford more trouble. He had already been summoned to Rome once, and the stakes for his own political survival were too high to risk protecting the life of one innocent man. Little did he suspect that this apparently small act of cowardice would become the only reason why he is remembered in history.

# THE EASTER MESSAGE

Easter is not as cozy as Christmas. At the heart of the Christmas story lies a baby, shepherds, animals, kings and presents. Easter in contrast talks about nails, blood, a crown of thorns and a man dying on a cross. Yet there is an astonishing message in Jesus' death on the cross. His suffering was not pointless; it was God's way of taking upon himself all the sin and evil of the world in order to forgive humanity. On the cross God says to us, 'Not only do I know about your suffering, I have shared in it.'

## PRAYERS FOR EASTER DAYS

### Lent

*Lord Jesus Christ,*
*You know what it is like to be tempted*
*For you were tempted in the wilderness;*
*You know how easy it is to do wrong things*
*And much harder to do the right way*
*You know too what it is*
*to be disappointed,*
*To be misunderstood,*
*To be let down by friends,*
*To be cruelly treated and put to death,*
*Yet able to forgive those who wronged you.*
*Please help us*
*Not to give in when we are tempted,*
*Not to be hurt by what others do.*

*Forgive us if in any way we have wronged you;*
*Help us to forgive those who wrong us;*
*And help us to follow your example.*
**Carol Watson**

### Palm Sunday

*Lord Jesus, I would like to have seen you when you rode into Jerusalem on the back of a donkey. I'd like to have been one of the crowd who cheered and shouted and sang glad songs of welcome to the king. Help me to welcome you today in my life and to know that you are always with me. Amen.*

## Maundy Thursday

On Maundy Thursday we remember
Christ's command to love one another.

*Lord, make me an instrument of*
*your peace.*
*Where there is hatred, let me sow*
*love,*
*Where there is injury, pardon,*
*Where there is despair, hope,*
*Where there is darkness, light,*
*Where there is sadness, joy.*
**Francis of Assisi**

*Teach us, Lord, to serve you as you*
*deserve,*
*To give and not to count the cost,*
*To fight and not to heed the*
*wounds,*
*To toil and not to seek for rest,*
*To labour and not to ask for any*
*reward*
*Save that of knowing that we do*
*your will.*
**Ignatius of Loyola**

## Good Friday

*Father of all,*
*we give you thanks and praise that*
*when we were far off you met us in*
*your Son and brought us home.*
**The Alternative Service Book**

*Dear Lord,*
*Thank you for dying for us, and*
*thank you for loving us even*
*though we do things wrong.*
*Amen.*
**Iona Miller (aged 11)**

*Be merciful to me, O God,*
*because of your constant love.*
*Because of your great mercy*
*wipe away my sins!*
*Wash away all my evil*
*and make me clean from my sin!*
*Remove my sin, and I will be*
*clean;*
*Wash me, and I will be whiter*
*than snow.*
**From Psalm 51**

## Easter Sunday

*God has raised from death our*
*Lord Jesus, who is the Great*
*Shepherd of the sheep ... May the*
*God of peace provide you with*
*every good thing you need in order*
*to do his will, and may he,*
*through Jesus Christ, do in us*
*what pleases him. And to Christ be*
*the glory for ever and ever!*
**Letter to the Hebrews, Good News Bible**

*Christ, we thank you for all our*
*rebirths. We thank you for*
*forgiveness and second chances,*
*both for ourselves and others.*
*This Easter season as sleeping*
*seeds and trees begin to burst into*
*new life, help us all to become*
*more alive and to grow more*
*nearly into the people you mean*
*us to be.*
**Avery Brooke**

Dear God

Thank you for all the Wonderful things
you've given me: a family, a happy home
lots of love, friends, food and clothes
I'm sorry I don't always get things
right, and some times quarrel with my
brother.

Thank you for Easter And the love
you Show us.

please let the Easter Bunny come.

Amen,

E is for Easter, coming again soon,

A is for angels near the tomb,

S is for stone which was rolled away

T is for Tomb found empty that day,

E is for early morning, the women are glad,

R is for the Risen Lord, no need to be sad

# MAKE AN EASTER GARDEN

It is a long-standing tradition among **Christians to prepare an Easter garden in Holy Week, to remember the garden tomb which the women visited early on Easter Sunday morning.**

### You need:

◇ A shallow tray or dish
◇ Garden soil or potting compost
◇ Moss, cut grass or sand
◇ Dried twigs
◇ Sewing thread
◇ Small pot
◇ Flat stone large enough to cover the mouth of the pot
◇ Egg cups (or other small containers)
◇ Small flowers
◇ Gravel

### To make:

1 Fill the tray with soil or potting compost.

2 Arrange it to make a hill on one side of the tray.

3 Cover the soil with moss, grass or sand.

4 Make three crosses with dried twigs tied together with sewing thread and place on the hilltop.

5 Press the small pot into the 'hillside' to make a cave like the garden tomb. Place the stone over the mouth of the tomb.

6 Press egg-cups full of water into the soil around the 'garden' and fill them with flowers.

7 Make a path coming from the tomb with gravel, to show how the disciples ran to the tomb on Easter morning.

8 Early on Easter morning, move back the stone from the tomb—showing that it is empty.

# Good Friday—the Crossroads of History

*The army officer who was standing there in front of the cross saw how Jesus had died. 'This man was really the Son of God!' he said.*

**The Gospel of Mark**

**Good Friday is the name given to the day when we remember Christ's crucifixion. Today the cross is perhaps the world's most famous symbol. It can be seen on flags and badges, in schools and art galleries, even on T-shirts, earrings or necklaces. To many people today the cross is a symbol of hope and comfort but in AD30 the cross meant one of the cruellest forms of death ever devised by human beings. The eyewitnesses to Jesus' last hours on the cross included a Roman soldier. He had been given the task of executing a criminal, but ended by recognizing Jesus' true identity as God's Son.**

## The centurion's story

I was in charge of the execution party that day. It's not a job I volunteer for. Soldiers can't be squeamish about death, but you always run the risk of things getting out of hand at these public crucifixions. Something about it seems to bring out the worst in people.

The prisoner had already been flogged when we bound the crossbeam to him. His back was red raw; it was obvious he would have trouble making it to the top of the hill carrying his cross. There was an unusually large crowd pressing in on us, some mouthing curses at the prisoner, and others—a group of women—wailing and weeping so that I could hardly hear myself speak. The prisoner actually paused to tell them to stop weeping. I took the chance to order a man in the crowd to carry the prisoner's cross the rest of the way to the hill.

The place is known as the Skull—for obvious reasons. There are always a few grim poles waiting there to receive the crossbeams with their human cargo. Today there were three. We had a couple of petty thieves to deal with as well as the prisoner.

The men know what to do. Each of the prisoners is stripped and his hands are nailed to the wood. The crossbeams are lifted into place and the feet also nailed down. I usually busy myself with the crowd while this is going on; it's not the kind of thing I enjoy watching.

We had been given a sign,

This is the King of the Jews

which was to hang over the prisoner's head by order of Pilate. It provoked a good deal of cackling and taunting among the crowd, 'If you're a king, why don't you save yourself?' they howled at him. Even one of the thieves spat out curses in between his screams of agony.

By now my men had sat down to gamble for the prisoner's robe. I turn a blind eye to the practice—in a job like this they need to have some perks. That was when I first took a proper look at the prisoner. I've seen many die this way; whatever dignity they possess soon deserts them when their sinews start to pull apart and the weight of the body becomes unbearable. But this one—no screams, no curses, only silence.

At one point he spoke and seemed to be praying. I know only a little Hebrew but it sounded like 'Father, forgive them.' Why would a man dying a hideous death say a thing like that?

By the ninth hour it had grown very dark. Many of the crowd had grown tired and gone home, apart from the women who remained watching silently at a distance. It's usual for all the prisoners to be unconscious by this time—a mercy to them since they pass into death unawares. But suddenly the prisoner raised his head and said quite distinctly: 'Father, into your hands I give my spirit.' Then he died. As if he wouldn't have his life taken from him but chose when to give it up himself.

They tell me his name was Jesus—the prisoner. I don't know if he really was a king—but I'll say this: he died like one.

## DARK FRIDAY OR GOOD FRIDAY?

*O strange and unspeakable mystery,*
*The judge was judged,*
*He who loosed the bound was bound,*
*He who created the world was fixed*
*    with nails,*
*He who measures heaven and earth was*
*    measured,*
*He who gives creatures life died,*
*He who raises the dead was buried.*
**Melito of Sardis**

The day on which Jesus was crucified has been remembered by Christians down the ages as Good Friday. But the name is a puzzle. On the face of it, the day when God's Son was cruelly murdered doesn't sound all that good. Dark Friday might be a more appropriate name.

Whether Good Friday deserves its name depends on your point of view. Jesus' followers didn't originally see it that way, and the Gospel records his mother's heartbreak at seeing her son die.

# CRUCIFIXION

Jesus was not the only person to die by crucifixion. Historians believe that the Persians were the first to use this barbaric and tortuous means of execution. In the Roman Empire crucifixion was a death for common criminals—slaves, murderers and terrorists among them. Jesus was sentenced for high treason as a political agitator and a pretender to the Emperor's throne.

There were several stages to the slow death of crucifixion. First the prisoner would be stripped and flogged using leather straps with teeth of bone, thorns or lead which would tear the flesh. Then the victim was nailed or bound to the horizontal beam of the cross which he was forced to carry to the place of execution. The vertical pole was already in place and the body and crossbeam would be lifted into place and secured. Finally the feet were nailed to the cross and the victim was left to await death.

Only Jesus himself seemed to know the real significance of that Friday. He had warned his followers several times what was going to happen, but none of them appeared to take it in.

Jesus' death appears in a completely different light once you accept that he chose deliberately to submit to it. His mission on earth wasn't cut short but actually reached its fulfilment in the suffering of the cross. Christians believe that Jesus stood in our place. His death paid the penalty not for his own wrongdoing but for ours. In the shadow of the cross is a mystery which perhaps can never be fully understood—through Jesus, God took responsibility on himself for the wrongdoing, pain and suffering of the world to make it new.

### MY SONG IS LOVE UNKNOWN

*My song is love unknown:*
*My saviour's love to me;*
*Love to the loveless shown,*
*That they might lovely be.*
*O who am I,*
*That for my sake*
*My Lord should take*
*Frail flesh, and die?*

*He came from his blest throne,*
*Salvation to bestow:*
*But men made strange and none*
*The longed-for Christ would know.*
*But O my friend!*
*My friend indeed*
*Who at my need his life did spend.*

*Sometimes they strew his way,*
*And His sweet praises sing:*
*Resounding all the day,*
*Hosannas to their King*
*Then: crucify!*
*Is all their breath,*
*And for his death*
*They thirst and cry.*

*They rise and needs will have*
*My dear Lord made away;*
*A murderer they save;*
*The Prince of life they slay.*
*Yet cheerful He*
*To suffering goes,*
*That He his foes*
*From thence might free.*
**Samuel Crossman 1624–83**

# GOOD FRIDAY FAVORITES

The name Good Friday may have once been God's Friday but in some European countries it is called Great Friday and in Denmark they remember Long Friday.

It is now a public holiday in most countries, but in times past some tradespeople, including miners, fishermen and blacksmiths, refused to work because it was thought to bring bad luck. Customs and superstitions associated with Good Friday range from playing marbles to planting seeds, but the custom that has survived best is undoubtedly the baking of hot cross buns. An old English rhyme from 1733 says:

*Good Friday comes this month,*
*The old woman runs*
*With one- or two-a-penny hot cross buns,*
*Whose virtue is, if you believe what's*
*said,*
*They'll not grow mouldy like the*
*common bread.*

Buns with a cross in the top are also a tradition in other European countries, such as Norway and Austria, but here is a recipe for the English version.

## HOT CROSS BUNS

### You need:

**Yeast liquid**
◇ 1 level tbsp dried yeast
◇ 1 tsp sugar
◇ 1/4 cup warm milk
◇ 2/3 cup warm water
◇ 3/4 cup plain flour

**Dough**
◇ 3 cups plain flour
◇ 1 level tsp salt
◇ 1 level tsp each mixed spice, cinnamon and nutmeg
◇ 1/4 cup sugar
◇ 1/4 cup butter, melted
◇ 1 egg, beaten
◇ 1/4 cup currants
◇ 1/4 cup mixed peel

**Glaze**
◇ 2 tbsp milk
◇ 2 tbsp sugar

### To make:

1 Blend in the yeast with the warm milk mixed with water, the sugar and flour. Leave for about 20–30 minutes in a warm place until frothy.

2 Sift together the remaining flour, salt, spices and sugar.

3 Stir the butter and egg into the yeast batter; gradually add flour and fruit. Mix well.

4 Knead the dough on floured board for about 10 minutes until smooth.

5 Divide your dough into 12 pieces and shape into buns. Place well apart on a floured baking sheet and cover with a cloth or large polythene bag. Leave to rise in a warm place for about 45 minutes, until doubled in size.

6 Make two slashes to form a cross on the top of each bun with a sharp knife.

7 Bake in a medium oven 375° F for 15–20 minutes or until they are golden brown.

8 To glaze: while the buns are still warm, bring the milk to the boil, stir in the sugar and boil for two minutes. Brush buns twice with the glaze.

# EASTER CAROLS

Everybody connects the word 'carols' with Christmas but in their heyday—1400 to the mid 1600s—carols were written for many feast days including Easter. Many of the best-loved tunes had new words written for them in the 1800s to convert them into Christmas carols.

The word carol originally meant 'dance in a ring', which suggests that these traditional folksongs were often meant to be accompanied by dancing.

The words of these two greatly-loved Easter hymns express the significance of Easter for Christians everywhere.

### WHEN I SURVEY

*When I survey the wondrous cross*
*On which the Prince of Glory died,*
*My richest gain I count but loss,*
*And pour contempt on all my*
*pride.*

*Forbid it, Lord, that I should*
*boast,*
*Save in the death of Christ my*
*God:*
*All the vain things that charm me*
*most,*
*I sacrifice them to his blood.*

*See from his head, his hands, his*
*feet,*
*Sorrow and love flow mingled*
*down:*

*Did e'er such love and sorrow*
*meet,*
*Or thorns compose so rich a crown?*

*Were the whole realm of nature*
*mine,*
*That were an offering far too*
*small,*
*Love so amazing, so divine,*
*Demands my life, my soul, my all.*
**Isaac Watts 1674–1748**

## THERE IS A GREEN HILL FAR AWAY

There is a green hill far away,
Without a city wall,
Where the dear Lord was crucified
Who died to save us all.


We may not know, we cannot tell
What pains he had to bear,
But we believe it was for us
He hung and suffered there.


He died that we might be forgiven,
He died to make us good;
That we might go at last to
  heaven,
Saved by his precious blood.

There was no other good enough
To pay the price of sin;
He only could unlock the gate
Of heaven and let us in.


O dearly, dearly has he loved,
And we must love him too,
And trust in his redeeming blood
And try his works to do.

**C.F. Alexander 1818–95**

# *A Time for Celebration*

*Mary of Magdala went to the disciples with the news: 'I have seen the Lord!'*

**The Gospel of John**

**Easter Day is the high point of the festival. A day for games, gift-giving and celebrating the gladdest news of all: that Christ rose from the dead and lives forever. The traditional Easter gift is the egg. Its shape reminds us of the tombstone that was rolled away and the secret it hides inside is of new life breaking into the world.**

**According to John's Gospel, the first person to meet the risen Jesus was Mary Magdalene (Mary of Magdala). She was one of the women who had followed Jesus all the way to Jerusalem from Galilee.**

## Mary Magdalene's story

We were up before daybreak. As we left the outskirts of Jerusalem, we could just see the first fingers of dawn warming the rooftops of the city. No one else was about. There was only the sound of our feet on the road and the sweet, heavy smell of the spices in the basket. There were three of us: Mary (James' mother), Salome and myself. The spices were for the body. We couldn't take them before because it was forbidden on the Sabbath.

As we made our way along the path to the garden we were talking about how we could get into the tomb. The entrance had been blocked with a great stone, too heavy even for three of us to move. Not only that, we'd heard the Romans had placed a guard at the entrance; we were afraid they might turn us away.

# MARY MAGDALENE

Mary Magdalene appears several times in the four Gospels. Magdala, a town in Galilee, is probably the root of her name. She is first mentioned by Luke as one of the women who travelled with Jesus and the disciples in their tour of Galilee's towns and villages. The group of women (Joanna, Mary the mother of James, and Salome are also named) worked with Jesus and his followers living out of their own means.

Luke tells us that Mary Magdalene had been healed by Jesus and this was probably when she began to follow him. Indeed, Mary followed Jesus all the way from her home to the cross and was the first to see him after his resurrection.

We reached the garden where the tomb was. What we saw made us stop dead in our tracks. There was the stone—but rolled away to one side with the entrance to the tomb gaping open. The guards were nowhere to be seen. We looked at each other, reading the fear in each other's eyes. Something terrible had happened.

Inside the tomb our fears were realized. There were the strips of linen which had been wrapped around the body—but no body. It had simply gone. Everything was still and silent. As if the world had stopped.

I was the first to move. I turned and ran back to the city and told Peter and the others what we'd seen. They looked at me as if I was raving. I don't think one of them believed me. But Peter and John came to see for themselves. Everything was just as we had left it.

When they had gone to tell the others, I remained behind in the garden. I wanted time to think about what had happened. I started crying. I went back inside the tomb to look again, and that was the first time I saw them. Two men (were they men?) sitting on the stone shelf where the body had once been—one at the head and one at the foot. They were clothed in white, and when one of them spoke his voice was like rain falling.

'Woman, why are you crying?'

'They've taken my Lord away,' I said, 'and I don't know where they have put him.'

Then there was someone else, standing behind me at the mouth of the tomb with the sharp morning light behind him. He asked me the same question.

'Woman, why are you crying? Who are you looking for?'

I thought he might be the gardener so I said: 'Sir, if you have taken him away, tell me where and I will come and get him.'

He stepped forward and said my name. Said it in a way I'd heard it spoken before.

'Mary.'

Then I knew who it was. No one had taken the body. It—he—was standing there before me. When or how I couldn't say. But this was my Lord, this was Jesus—alive.

# THE FIRE AND THE LIGHT

On Easter Day, Christians all over the world welcome the rising of Jesus from the dead. The dark days of his trial and crucifixion are behind, and now is the time to celebrate the light of life dawning and Christ's victory over the powers of death and darkness. In churches from the West to the East this is demonstrated dramatically in Easter services. Customs vary from country to country but usually the celebration symbolizes passing from darkness to light.

Often the church building has been stripped of all decoration since Maundy Thursday and the inside is cloaked in darkness. The congregation gathers around the entrance to the church as Easter Day dawns. Then the priest strikes sparks of fire from a piece of flint and lights one huge candle—known as the Paschal candle. Fire and light are used to show the power and glory of the Savior rising to life.

The Paschal candle is carried into the church and used to light other smaller candles on stands or held in people's hands. Children's wondering faces watch the light spread around the church until the whole building, dark before, is filled with warm, dancing candlelight. Then the church can be decorated with flowers for Easter morning; color is everywhere, the bells are rung, and Easter Day has come again.

# LIGHTING THE WORLD

Easter celebrations assume a different form in each part of the world. One popular custom is the sunrise service, usually held in the open air at dawn on Easter Sunday.

In America, sunrise services have been held for many years in the spectacular National Parks, including the Grand Canyon. At Aspen, Colorado, worshippers travel by ski-lift to a service on the top of the 11,300ft Ajax mountain. On the West coast thousands gather for the service in the Hollywood Bowl in California. The first service there was held over sixty years ago and traditionally includes a symphony orchestra and a large choir to sing the Easter hymns.

In some parts of Germany the tradition is to light bonfires on hilltops during Easter eve. People come from the surrounding towns and villages to gather round the fires, playing games and singing hymns. In the Harz mountains an old custom exists where giant oak wheels, as large as two yards in diameter, are pushed to the top of a hill. The wheels are stuffed with straw which is set on fire. Then the giant firework is rolled downhill into the valley. The fields where it comes to rest are considered to be specially blessed and likely to yield a rich crop at harvest-time.

Nowhere is Easter more vividly celebrated than in Russia. In the Orthodox church, now free from the watchful eye of Communism, midnight mass is a moving and dramatic pageant. The priest approaches the main door of the church and echoes the words of Mary Magdalene:

'They have taken my Lord away and I know not where they have laid him.'

The words of the angel come in answer: 'Whom do you seek?'

'The body of Jesus.'

'He is not here, he is risen—*Khristos voskrese!*'

The words are answered by the congregation. *'Voistinu voskrese!* He is risen indeed.' And the candle flame, the light of Christ, passes from believer to believer as it has done for centuries past.

# EASTER EGGS

Eggs and Easter go together like carols and Christmas. No one knows when the egg was first used as a symbol in festivals. Egg painting goes back at least 3,000 years in China, Greece and the Ancient East. Eggs were given as gifts in spring festivals. In India it was believed that the earth was created by a golden egg which shone like the sun and split itself in two.

For Christians, the egg is a symbol of Jesus' resurrection, of new life breaking through the hard shell of the tomb. Inside is the secret of life—a new creation which any person can receive through faith in Christ and the power of his resurrection.

Christians probably adopted the egg as a symbol early in the history of Easter. An Armenian illuminated manuscript from the year 1038 shows the women at the empty tomb. On the stone sits an angel who points to a large white egg bearing the words: *He is not here, he is risen.*

In the English Middle Ages kings would give eggs as presents, sometimes richly decorated in gold leaf. In other countries red is the traditional color for the egg, possibly as a reminder that Christ gave his lifeblood for humanity.

Today eggs are still painted in many countries. The first 'sweet' egg, made from marzipan and sugar, was introduced around one hundred years ago. Since then chocolate eggs have become a favorite with most children.

## Egg-shaped games

All sorts of games are played with Easter eggs. They are hidden in baskets, hunted,

rolled, and even thrown.

Children in France throw their eggs in the air and catch them. The first player to drop an egg is the loser. In Greece, decorated eggs are carried to church. When two people meet, they knock their eggs together and greet each other: 'Christ is risen.'

Egg rolling is popular in many countries. In Washington DC, USA, the Easter Monday custom of egg rolling outside the White House was introduced by the President's wife in 1877. One visitor described an early egg rolling like this:

*The children sit sedately in long rows; each has brought a basket of bright colored, hard boiled eggs, and those on the upper terrace send them rolling to the line on the next below, and these pass on the ribbon-like streams to other hundreds at the foot, who scramble for the hopping eggs and hurry panting to the top to start them down again. And as the sport warms up, those on top who have rolled all the eggs they brought finally roll themselves down, shrieking with laughter.*

The annual Easter egg rolling is still held today on slopes in view of the White House.

## Rich eggs

The most costly eggs of all were undoubtedly the ones made by Carl Fabergé, the great Russian goldsmith and jeweller. Fabergé lived in St Petersburg during the time of the Tsars. His Easter eggs were fabulous creations studded with pearls and diamonds. The first was made for the Tsar Alexander III to present to the Tsarina. Often Fabergé's eggs would open to reveal more treasures inside such as a hen with ruby eyes or a replica of the Imperial Coronation coach. Sadly, when the Russian Revolution took place, Fabergé was exiled from his country and died in Lausanne in Switzerland in 1920.

## Decorating eggs

Chocolate eggs for eating can be bought in most countries today. But the custom of decorating real eggs goes back thousands of years and can still be fun at Easter.

There are various ways of coloring eggs—some easy, some more time-consuming—but all of them can be done by children with a little help from an adult. Here are three to choose from.

## EGG HEADS

**A simple method of decorating an egg that any child can enjoy.**

### You need:

◇ Several eggs
◇ Scraps of material: cloth, ribbon, cotton or net
◇ Poster paints
◇ An egg carton
◇ Cardboard

### To make:

1  Hard-boil two or three eggs to use. Bring to the boil and simmer for about twenty minutes. Then let them cool. (Make sure an adult helps with this part.)

2  Cut out the cone part from an egg carton to act as the body for your egg head. Make a hole in the top for the egg to sit in.

3  Paint a face design on your egg with poster paints. It can be a clown, an Easter rabbit or a man or woman.

4  Cover the body with material. Add a ribbon bow or a hat made from a painted egg carton cone. The white rabbit can be covered thinly with cotton for fur, cutting ears from cardboard.

## DELICATE DESIGNS

This method produces brightly colored dyed eggs with delicate patterns on them.

### You need:

◇ Eggs (hard-boiled)
◇ Fabric or vegetable dye
◇ Small leaves, blades of grass, petals or pressed flowers
◇ Vegetable oil
◇ Nylon stockings or pantyhose

### To make:

1 Dip the leaves, petals or flowers in the vegetable oil. Then stick them onto the egg's surface in whatever pattern you like.

2 Wrap the egg tightly in a piece of stocking and tie at the top with thread so that the leaves are pressed onto the shell.

3 Dye the egg in the fabric or vegetable dye, following the instructions on the packet.

4 Remove the stocking and the pieces you stuck on. The colored egg will have the outline of the plants in delicate imprint on the shell.

## FABULOUS FABERGÉ EGG

You may not be able to afford real pearls and diamonds to decorate this egg but it can still look dazzling. If you cut the top off, the egg also makes a pretty jewellery box—but make sure an adult does the cutting.

### You need:

◇ A goose egg
◇ Rubber band
◇ Sharp craft knife
◇ Bowl to hold the egg's contents
◇ Nail polish—bright pink or purple
◇ Strong adhesive
◇ Decorations—fake jewellery, gold braid, sequins
◇ Napkin ring or candle holder for base

### To make:

1 To make a lid at the top of the egg, first put a rubber band over the pointed end about one third of the way down; mark a guideline with a pencil. Remove the rubber band and cover the guideline with transparent tape to reinforce it. With the craft knife cut with repeated light strokes, working through the egg a bit at a time. Leave the contents inside while cutting, but make sure you have a bowl ready to catch them.

2  Clean the inside of the egg with water and shake it dry.

3  Paint the egg with several coats of glossy nail polish.

4  Finally decorate with your own design. Glue on the gold braid first and then add plastic pearls, beads or rows of threaded sequins. A final touch can be added with a jewel brooch on the top.

5  Mount the egg on a napkin ring or candle holder using glue to attach it.

# A TWIST IN THE TALE

It's easy when reading the Easter story today to think that Jesus' followers were only waiting for him to rise from the dead. The truth is that, despite Jesus' predictions of what had to happen, the disciples were convinced after his crucifixion, death and burial that they would never see him again.

At the time of the resurrection they were stunned and frightened, huddled together behind locked doors for fear that the Roman authorities who had killed their leader might be looking for them as well.

When the women returned from the tomb with the news that Jesus was alive, nobody rejoiced; they simply didn't believe them.

People today who doubt the truth of Jesus' resurrection could hardly be more doubtful than some of Jesus' own followers, who included hard-headed fishermen and a tax officer. If they were to believe in a man rising from the grave, they would have to see it with their own eyes. And that is exactly what happened.

Jesus appeared not just once—to Mary Magdalene—but to all eleven disciples together, and on another occasion to 500 amazed witnesses. The event that launched Christianity upon the world was not a carefully stage-managed rumor. It was a shock, a twist in the tale that not even Jesus' closest friends had expected.

## The Ballad of the Bread Man

*He went round to all the people*
*A paper crown on his head.*
*Here is some bread from my father.*
*Take, eat, he said.*

*Nobody seemed very hungry.*
*Nobody seemed to care.*
*Nobody saw the god in himself*
*Quietly standing there.*

*He finished up in the papers.*
*He came to a very bad end.*
*He was charged with bringing the*
*    living to life.*
*No man was that prisoner's friend.*

*There's only one kind of punishment*
*To fit that kind of crime.*
*They rigged a trial and shot him dead.*
*They were only just in time.*

*They lifted the young man by the leg,*
*They lifted him by the arm,*
*They locked him in a cathedral*
*In case he came to harm.*

*They stored him safe as water*
*Under seven rocks.*
*One Sunday morning he burst out*
*Like a jack-in-the-box.*

*Through the town he went walking.*
*He showed them the holes in his head.*
*Now do you want any loaves? he*
*    cried.*
*'Not today,' they said.*

**Charles Causley**

# *E*aster Everlasting

*Though the doors were locked, Jesus came and stood among them, and said, 'Peace be with you!' Then he said to Thomas, 'Put your finger here; see my hands . . . Stop doubting and believe.'*

*Thomas answered, 'My Lord and my God.'*

**The Gospel of John**

**The Easter season does not stop on Easter Day. Officially it goes on for six weeks until Whit Sunday or Pentecost, when God sent the Holy Spirit as Jesus had promised. It was probably once known as White Sunday because of the white robes that newly-baptized Christians wore in procession.**

**For the first followers of Jesus, Easter Sunday morning was only the beginning. The shock of the empty tomb was the first of many surprises. Jesus appeared to his disciples on a number of different occasions after that. Not all found it easy to believe that such a miracle could occur. Thomas the Twin, one of the twelve disciples, is known as 'doubting Thomas' because of his reluctance to accept what had happened.**

## Thomas' story

To me it sounded as if they'd all lost their grip on reality. Admittedly we'd all been under a strain since Jesus died. Skulking indoors in constant fear of arrest is enough to put anyone's nerves on edge. Few of us went outside except under the cover of darkness. We kept the doors locked at all times.

There wasn't much to talk about except what had happened, how we'd all expected so much from Jesus, and how all our hopes had been dashed in such a sudden, cruel, ugly way. Well, it was natural to wish Jesus would come back to us—but to imagine it had actually happened—I had more sense than that!

I'd gone out that Sunday evening after dark to get some food for us all. When I got back, the others were all in a state of feverish excitement. Jesus had been there they said, had suddenly appeared in the room among them. He'd shown them his hands and his side and spoken to them. No matter how much I reasoned with them, they kept repeating the same story. Finally I told them, 'Unless I see the nail marks in his hands and put my finger where the nails were, and put my hand into his side, I won't believe it.'

A week later we were in the same room with the doors bolted. I'd been watching for intruders from a window. I turned to say something to Peter and saw his face had gone deathly pale. I followed his gaze. Jesus was standing in the room. Nobody moved or dared to breathe. He greeted us in his familiar way: 'Peace be with you.'

Then he turned to me and held out his hands. 'Come, Thomas, put your finger here, see my hands. Reach out your hand and put it into my side. Stop doubting and believe.'

I took half a step forward—not knowing what to do. I found myself down on my knees saying, 'My Lord and my God.' I think if he'd asked me to do anything at that moment, even give up my own life, I would have done it.

Jesus said to me, 'Do you believe because you have seen me? How happy are those who believe without seeing me.'

Was I ashamed? Yes. But I was also happy beyond words. I had been proved utterly wrong and I've never been so glad to admit it.

# HOLIDAY GAMES AND CUSTOMS

It is hardly surprising that in Christian countries the days following Easter should be time for a holiday and celebrations. After all, without Easter there would be no Christian faith!

In the past, the Monday and Tuesday after Easter were called Hocktide, and celebrated with many games and sports. Today public holidays following Easter Day are often marked by football matches, horse or motor racing and all kinds of fairs and entertainments.

## Bonnets and bows

The Easter season was once the occasion for many strange and wonderful customs. When the Greek King Constantine was on the throne, he commanded that his subjects walk through the countryside wearing their best clothes out of respect for Jesus. Hundreds of years later the custom survived in people wearing some new item of clothing for Easter Day—even if it were only a shoelace or a new ribbon in the hair. A pair of gloves sent to a girl at Easter meant her suitor had serious intentions. If the girl put them on then wedding bells were almost certain!

Easter bonnets were popular in Britain until quite recently and ladies used to stroll in London's Battersea Park to show off their new hats. Nowadays the Easter bonnet parade has become a procession, complete with bands and floats. New York's Fifth Avenue is another place where bystanders can see new Easter clothes on parade.

In Eastern Europe, Easter Monday was once known as 'Ducking Monday' when unmarried girls had cause to beware in case they were thrown into ponds and lakes. If no ponds were nearby then a bucket of water would do the job. To add insult to the injury, the girls were informed that this custom would make them better wives!

Easter Monday and Tuesday used to be the occasion for the custom of 'heaving' in England. A Shrewsbury gentleman writes in 1799:

*I was sitting alone last Easter Tuesday at breakfast when I was surprised by the entrance of all the female servants of the house handing in an armchair, lined with white and decorated with ribbons and favours of all different colours. I asked them what they wanted. Their answer was that they came to heave me. It was the custom of that place on that morning, and they hoped I would take a seat in the chair...*

Heaving consisted of lifting the seated person three times high in the air, after which they could pay a small price to be released. This originally gentle custom got out of hand when gangs of young men started to seize strangers and toss them into the air, refusing to let them go until they had paid. Magistrates unsuccessfully tried to ban heaving.

Skittles, stoolball and handball were popular games all over Europe during the holiday season. Today's Easter sports and games seem positively tame by comparison!

# COLORS OF EASTER

*O little bulb uncouth*
*Ragged and rusty brown*
*Have you some dew of youth*
*Have you a rusty gown?*
*Plant me and see*
*What I shall be—*
*God's fine surprise*
*Before your eyes.*
**Maltbie D. Babcock**

On Good Friday, churches are traditionally
bare and empty but with the dawn of Easter
Day they become blazes of color. Flowers of
all kinds herald the joy of Christ's risen
presence.

In Europe, Easter falls in springtime
when there are a great variety of spring
blooms to choose from. In Sweden the
custom is to bring budding branches of trees
into the house before Easter so that they will
flower during the festival. The branches
may become an Easter tree hung with
painted eggs or, in Norway, decorated with
colored feathers.

Bowls of golden daffodils, crocuses or
sweet-smelling hyacinths are often given as
Easter gifts in Britain while in America a
special Easter-flowering lily has been
imported from Bermuda.

Lilies are also a traditional flower in
Australia where Easter comes in Autumn
and brings daisies and early
chrysanthemums in gold, red, pink or
white. The Easter colors—purple, blue,
gold and white—all have their own special
significance.

◇ Purple—the color for Lent and the
color of kings. At one time only the rich
could afford to wear purple because the
precious dye was found only in a small
shellfish found in the Mediterranean
Sea. The purple orchis is sometimes
called 'Gethsemane' because its spotted
leaves were said to be stained with
Christ's blood. Other purple flowers are
violets, hyacinths, irises, lilac and
crocuses.

◇ Blue—the color associated with Jesus'
mother, Mary. Legend has it that the
pretty blue speedwell grew on the road
Jesus walked on the way to Calvary.
Anemones, cornflowers, grape
hyacinths and irises can also be blue.

◇ White—the color of purity and joy.
Easter candles are usually white, and
the early Christians wore white robes
for baptism to show that their sins had
been washed away by Christ's
forgiveness. Lilies, tulips, narcissi and
crocuses are other white flowers.

◇ Yellow—the color of the sun,
connected with new life and rebirth.
Daffodils, chrysanthemums, crocuses,
lilies and branches of forsythia can be
used in arrangements where yellow is
the dominant color.

# FLOWER DECORATIONS

### HANGING EGG BASKETS

**A delicate miniature hanging basket can be made using an eggshell filled with tiny flowers.**

### You need:

◇ An egg
◇ Poster paints
◇ Length of bright ribbon
◇ Small flowers—for example violets, crocuses or freesias

### To make:

1 Break off the top of the egg close to the smaller end and remove the contents. Straighten the broken edges of the egg.

2 Wash the egg carefully and check that it hasn't any cracks that would leak water.

3 Cut a piece of ribbon to a length to go right round the open edge of the egg. Glue it on so that about a third of the ribbon overlaps inside the egg.

4 Now take a second, longer length of ribbon for the handle. Pass it under the egg and glue it on both sides.

5 Fill the egg about half full with water and add the small flowers.

6 Tie the ends of the ribbon in a bow, hanging it on your Easter tree or elsewhere in the house.

## PRETTY AS A PICTURE

**Easter blooms may soon be past, but their beauty can be captured in a pressed flower picture. These make lovely birthday cards or gifts and are much easier to make than you may think.**

### You need:

◇ White blotting paper
◇ Clear tape
◇ Absorbent paper
◇ Some heavy books
◇ A variety of small flowers
◇ Colored card for backing
◇ Self-sealing clear plastic or glass picture frame

### To make:

1 Place the flowers on a piece of clean blotting paper and hold them down with one or two small pieces of clear tape over the stems.

2 Place a piece of absorbent paper over the flowers and then cover with another piece of blotting paper on top. Lay a few more flowers on the blotting paper and continue in this order until you've several layers of pressed flowers.

3 Cover with a final piece of blotting paper. Place some heavy books on top and store like this for at least three weeks.

4 When the flowers are pressed, arrange them in a pattern on the card (choose the background color to suit your flowers). Put a small amount of glue on the back of each flower and press gently down. Leave to dry for an hour.

5 To make a greeting card, cover the flowers with some self-sealing clear plastic. Or put the card in a glass frame to present as a gift.

# EASTER
# EVERLASTING

When the beautiful painted eggs are put away and the chocolate eggs are all eaten, what is left of Easter? Does the story of a man who was killed and came back to life 2,000 years ago really make any difference to us today?

To the first followers of Jesus, the resurrection on Easter Sunday morning certainly changed everything. The frightened and miserable people that hid behind locked doors after Jesus' death were altogether different by the day of Pentecost.

On that day Jesus kept the promise that he'd made them before returning to heaven. The Holy Spirit came to live within his followers, and they began spreading the message of Jesus' love and forgiveness for humankind.

Today the same message has reached millions of people throughout the world—Christians in Europe, Australia, China, Africa, America and beyond, who are united by their experience of the way Jesus still changes lives today.

The message of Easter is that God has not remained hidden. He came down to earth to show us what he is like in his Son, Jesus. Not only that, but, through Jesus' death on the cross, he did something to rescue humanity from all the wrong, evil and suffering in the world.

The events of the first Easter were

not just important 2,000 years ago; they have an everlasting significance. For, in the words of Easter Sunday morning, 'Christ is not dead, he is risen,' and he continues to live in the lives of all those who find him and put their faith in him.

An English country curate writes of Easter morning:

*I rose early and went out in the fresh brilliant morning between six and seven o'clock. The sun had already risen some time, but the grass was still white with the hoar frost. I walked across the common in the bright, sunny quite empty morning, listening to the rising of the lark as he went up in an ecstasy of song into the blue unclouded sky and gave in his Easter morning hymn at heaven's gate. Then came the echo and answer of earth as the Easter bells rang out their joy peals from the church towers all round. It was very sweet and lovely, the bright silent sunny morning, and the lark rising and singing alone in the blue sky, and then suddenly the morning air all alive with music of sweet bells ringing for the joy of the resurrection. 'The Lord is risen,' smiled the sun, 'The Lord is risen,' sang the lark. And the church bells in their joyous pealing answered from tower to tower, 'He is risen indeed.'*
**From Francis Kilvert's** *Diary*

# *Index*